Cold Spots:
Ghosts of San Antonio

Scott A. Johnson

Schiffer Publishing Ltd

4880 Lower Valley Road, Atglen, Pennsylvania 19310

Other Schiffer Books on Related Subjects:

San Antonio: Past, Present, & Always,
978-0-7643-3040-7, $24.99

*Ghosts of Fort Worth: Investigating Cowtown's
Most Haunted Locations,*
978-0-7643-2813-8, $14.95

*The Ghosts of Austin: Who They Are and
Where to Find Them,*
978-0-7643-2680-6, $14.95

Designed by Stephanie Daugherty
Type set in Rosemary Roman/NewsGoth BT

ISBN: 978-0-7643-3122-0

Printed in China

Schiffer Books are available at special
discounts for bulk purchases for sales
promotions or premiums. Special editions,
including personalized covers, corporate
imprints, and excerpts can be created in
large quantities for special needs. For more
information contact the publisher:

Published by Schiffer Publishing Ltd.
4880 Lower Valley Road
Atglen, PA 19310
Phone: (610) 593-1777
Fax: (610) 593-2002
E-mail: Info@schifferbooks.com

For the largest selection of fine reference
books on this and related subjects, please
visit our web site at:
www.schifferbooks.com
We are always looking for people to write
books on new and related subjects. If you
have an idea for a book please contact us at
the above address.

This book may be purchased from the
publisher.Include $5.00 for shipping.
Please try your bookstore first.You may
write for a free catalog.

In Europe, Schiffer books are distributed by
Bushwood Books
6 Marksbury Ave.
Kew Gardens
Surrey TW9 4JF England
Phone: 44 (0) 20 8392-8585; Fax: 44 (0)
20 8392-9876
E-mail: info@bushwoodbooks.co.uk
Website: www.bushwoodbooks.co.uk
Free postage in the U.K., Europe; air mail
at cost.

Printed in China

Dedication

It is with the deepest respect that this book is dedicated to the 189 proud Texans and more than 1,500 brave Mexicans who fought at the Battle of the Alamo in 1836. Although they are gone, their sacrifice will never be forgotten.

Also, to my wife and daughters, thank you for your continued love and support. Without you, there would be no me.

Acknowledgements

A book such as this one is not written by a lone person, but by an entire community. The stories contained herein are not simply tales of ghostly activity, but are the very lifeblood that gives a city its personality. Finding all these places would be impossible for a single person, and it's through the love and support of family and friends, colleagues and cohorts, that such a volume is written. The author would therefore like to thank the following:

First, to Tabatha, Anna, and Zoe, for sharing in my passions and allowing me the time to indulge in this macabre pastime. To Addison and Nancy, Brad and Jennifer, Zach and Vincent for lending your love and support. Thanks also to Clint and Heather McCrocklin, Matt Taylor, and Hoshi Aona, my fellow members of CSPR, for accompanying me to some really creepy locations into which no sane person would ever venture. Also, to Tiff Wheiles, for playing tour guide and chauffer.

Also, to Docia Schultz-Williams, Ernesto Malacara, Deborah Martin, Gus Gonzalez, Amy Fulkerson, and Rhett Rushing for taking so much of your busy time answering questions, and without whom the history of some of the most incredible locations in the city might have been lost.

Finally, special thanks must go to Steve "Uncle Creepy" Barton, Johnny Butane, Debbi Moore, Nomad, Ryan, Emmy, Emma, Buz, Kryton, Morgan, Dean, Melissa, David, Foy, Splat, and everyone else with Dread Central for giving me a voice to talk about this subject. Your continued support and friendship inspires and encourages me.

Contents

Introduction

D o you believe in ghosts? It's a question I ask often whenever I speak at schools or conventions. The crowds are usually an even split of believers and die-hard skeptics. In the end, it never really is a question of what a person believes, or whether or not I can convince anyone that ghosts are real or not. It all comes down to a personal choice that has to be made based on a person's experiences. Many times I've heard "Just wait until *it* happens to you." For some, "it" never does. What most can agree on, however, is that certain places, whether haunted or not, are downright creepy. They exist everywhere, in every country, state, county, city, and neighborhood. What they bring out of people is one of the most primal emotions, and one that everyone can share as a common experience: Fear. Through all my travels and research as a ghost hunter, whenever I talk to groups, I inevitably get that one question: "Don't you get scared?" While I'd like to say that I've never been frightened in my life, it simply isn't true. Sure, I get scared, but I'm the type who likes the feeling. It fascinates me. And nothing is more frightening, or fascinating, than the unknown. It is for this reason that, among my friends, there exists a joke that, were our lives a horror movie, I, being the one who goes off looking for the source of the strange noise or wants to investigate the basement, would probably be the first to die.

Texas pride is something unique in the United States, and nowhere is it more apparent than in San Antonio. This city is, after all, the birthplace of the rallying cry of "Remember the Alamo." From such beginnings, the city grew to a thriving center where many cultures meet and blend, giving San Antonio a flavor unique even in Texas. From the historic missions to the modern day Riverwalk restaurants, San Antonio is truly a city of wonders that can steal the breath away.

However, despite its charm and modern trappings, visitors should never forget the city's history. While tragedies have occurred since man first set foot on its soil, it is March 6, 1836 that will forever stand out in the memories of scholars and history buffs — that's the day 189 proud Texans defended a tiny mission against more than 1,500 Mexican soldiers, forever staining the ground with blood and pride. It was not the first tragedy on this land, nor was it the last. It was, however, a turning point in the history of the state, instilling in Texans a sense of honor whenever the battle is mentioned, even more so for those who can trace their lineage back to that fateful day. Wherever emotions run high, wherever people fought and died, and wherever lives have been lost or irrevocably changed, something is left behind. Whether it's in the form of bullet holes in a mud-brick wall or apparitions of those long since passed who just can't seem to rest, the scars of the past still remain.

Unlike the wonderful books of authors like Docia Schultz Williams, this book cannot begin to tell the whole story of the city. In fact, hundreds of books have been written purporting to do just that, yet most miss the mark, if even by just a little. A person could spend their entire lives researching this city, and still not know all there is to know about her rich culture and amazing history. Instead, this book serves another, decidedly more macabre, purpose. It serves as a sort of tour guide to the places in the city where the shadows are just a little darker, where the breezes that nip at the back of one's neck are not caused by a vent or fan, and where the dead still whisper. The places in this book hold the curious distinction of being...*haunted*.

Those who often look into haunted places may find this book missing a few items; some hotels or restaurants, maybe a house or two. The reasons for these purposeful omissions are varied, but can be summed up in a few simple sentences. In some cases the haunted locations may simply not exist anymore. With no trace, and no way to locate the elusive location, the item was left out. In other cases, the hauntings seem to have stopped. As the purpose of this book is to direct people to active spots, it seems that to add an inactive haunt would be to betray the reader. A few places that are reportedly haunted are not easily accessible to the public, making their inclusion in this book unnecessary. In most cases, however, certain places have been omitted at the request of those who now own them. Some people do not like to point out their properties' haunted histories, for whatever reason, and their wishes should be respected and the families left undisturbed.

Although the sites listed herein are still considered "active," ghosts are not trained beagles. They neither appear on command, nor do they do tricks. Despite the author's attempt to establish a best time or place for an encounter, there are no guarantees of seeing an apparition—no matter what time of day or year one visits these places. The best way to experience San Antonio, or any other city for that matter, is to take in the sights, talk to the people, sample the flavors, and really get a feel for the culture without getting overly concerned with whether or not you might see a ghost. Also, in most of the places highlighted, the history of the location alone is enough to be considered awe-inspiring. Enjoy the culture, the history, and the food. If the traveler is lucky, however, and the spirits of San Antonio take a liking, one might just go home with more than a few souvenirs. One might just go home with stories of when the dead in Texas told their tales.

1

Haunted Eateries, Meeting Places, & Bars

When visiting San Antonio, people begin to realize how vastly diverse its population is. Strolling past the restaurants on the Riverwalk, one is treated to scents from every culture, each one just as mouth-watering as the last. As the hot Texas sun beats down and fades into warm San Antonio nights, there is a great deal to be said for places where the drinks are always cold and plentiful and the food always hits the spot.

Like many other places in the city, there are things in the restaurants that are not on the menu, and the term "*spirits*" may not always be referring to the kind found in a bottle. In some places, old owners refuse to leave and past tragedies play themselves out over and over again, making the patron wonder if they'd had too much to drink, or just what was in the green sauce. Places like these are numerous in cities like San Antonio, where battles determined the future of a proud state and personalities had the reputation for being huge and flamboyant, and finding them is not at all difficult. In fact, some times, all a person has to do is follow his nose.

Victoria's Black Swan Inn

1006 Holbrook Road
San Antonio, TX 78218

Victoria's Black Swan Inn. *Courtesy of Bradford and Jennifer Johnson.*

The bride stands ready, her back to the crowd, as she prepares to throw the bouquet. Such a lovely old building and the wonderful arrangements have made her feel as she should on this, her special day: Like a queen. Yet as she raises her arm to let her flowers fly, she hesitates, unsure of what she's just seen. There, crossing the lawn, passed another woman in white...another bride. She watches as the woman makes a slow, carefree path down the hill toward the gazebo, where the woman in white, then, simply *disappears*.

There have been other strange things here, to be sure. Shadows darting away in periphery, guests that the bride didn't quite recognize, but far from being frightened, she feels what the bride in the gazebo feels. This place, this house...is full of love.

There are times in a person's life when everything must be perfect. The food must please the palate, the staff must be courteous, and the setting, too, must be beautiful. When the perfect location is found, it's easy to see why a person would never want to leave. In some places, that which haunts the location is not malevolent, is not angry, and did not die a violent death. What is left behind is the care that went into building a place, the strong work ethic of those who put their lives into making the place a home, and, most importantly, the love, not only of the people inside, but of the house itself.

The History

Where most homes and buildings date back as far as a hundred years or so, the land is seemingly ageless. Land, unless it was a battlefield, typically has little or no history before someone came and erected a structure on it. The history of Victoria's Black Swan Inn, however, stretches back much further, to around 5500 B.C. That is the estimated age of the oldest artifacts found on the site from a Native American culture that, at one point, thrived on what is now known as Saledo Creek.

For one reason or another, the tribe moved on or died out, leaving the land untamed for more than a century, until 1842. On September 19, the banks saw a horrifying battle that lasted only forty-five minutes, but which led to the deaths of more than sixty Mexican soldiers and the wounding of more than sixty more. Their opponents in the skirmish, a group of angry Texans, suffered only one casualty and only one man wounded.

Nearly thirty-five years later, a dairy farm was opened on the site by German immigrant Henrich Mahler. The farm served dual purposes, as he and his wife, Marie, began their family there, having four children. When she died in 1923, Henrich was devastated. He followed his beloved only two years later, leaving the house to his two sons, Daniel and Sam. The home was sold a few years later to two couples named Holbooks and Woods; the wives were sisters. They were to live in the home together and begin their families. They remodeled the house to make it suitable for two growing families and called it "White Gables." The Woods had a daughter, Joline, who, when she came of age, married a gentleman named Hall Park Street, an attorney in young San Antonio.

When her father, aunt, and uncle died within a short time of each other, Joline and her husband moved into White Gables to care for her mother. It was during this time that her husband, whom friends called "Park," became friends with novelist Earle Stanley Gardner. It has been theorized that Gardner may have based his popular "Perry Mason" character on Park, to whom the entire series is dedicated.

Joline Street died of cancer at the age of thirty-eight, devastating her husband. Though he remarried, even remaining in the home with his mother-in-law, he never truly got over the loss. On August 4, 1965, Hall Park Street hung himself from the poster of his bed with his belt, leaving the elderly Mrs. Woods with only her servants to care for her and a few devoted grandchildren. She died in her room shortly thereafter.

Mrs. Ingeborg Mehren purchased the house a few years later and refurbished it. She was the first to notice *strange* goings on in the house. It was sold a few other times before finally landing in the hands of Anne Rivera in the early 1990s.

The Ghosts...

Victoria's Black Swan Inn has been featured on several programs about hauntings and been investigated many times by various ghost-hunting groups, all of whom came to the same conclusion: *that there are many presences in the building*. In addition to cold spots, lights that flicker, and strange noises, there are other phenomena that some find unsettling at first.

Several caretakers have quickly left their positions after experiencing strange things in the house. The most common phenomenon is the sound of music, as if from an antique music box, that follows people through the house. Complemented by the sound of a piano playing when the house is empty, the auditory anomalies prompted at least one hearty caretaker to comment that she liked working there because the music was nice.

There are also several apparitions that have been reported by guests, customers, and employees alike. In one upstairs bedroom, a beautiful woman is often seen sitting. She has been identified as Mrs. Woods from when she was younger. In a smaller bedroom downstairs many people feel a "heaviness," as if the room itself oozes sadness. It was in this room that Mrs. Woods was confined in her later days, fearful that she would have to leave her beloved home. It was also in this room that she died.

There is also the presence of an angry looking man who has been seen all over the house. He is not alone, as other people have identified a second man from photographs as Park Street. The kitchen even seems to be inhabited by an older woman who has been identified as Marie Mahler, the home's original owner.

The two most commonly sighted – and talked about – apparitions are a child spirit who enjoys playing with dolls, pulling pranks, and throwing tantrums when other children are around, and a woman in white who is seen walking from the main house to the gazebo. Though the identity of the first one is unknown, the lady in white is thought to be Joline Street.

Present Day

Present Day Victoria's Black Swan Inn is an "inn" in name only, as it now functions more as a place where important events occur. Weddings, receptions and parties are held there, as are teatimes for a very special group of ladies. In 1996, the inn was featured on the television program "Sightings," during which a psychic made contact with several of the building's residents, and in 2005, the paranormal investigation group Psy Tech Kentucky stayed the night. Among their findings were numerous recordings of voices, including one that distinctly calls out the name "Joline." They had many personal experiences. While most of the spirits in the house are unpredictable, the spirit of Park Street has been sighted on the anniversary of his death. The best time to visit Victoria's Black Swan Inn, however, is when the event must be unforgettable. To book your party or event, call 210-590-2507. For more information, visit its web site at http://www.sawhost.com/victoriasblackswaninn/about_us.htm.

The Church Bistro & Theater
at King William

**1150 South Alamo Street
San Antonio, TX 78210**

The Church Bistro and Theater at King William

In the hush of a theater, an actor waits for his cue. Opening night jitters have firm hold of him, but, as the saying goes, the show must go on. Out of the corner of his eye, he spies what he at first takes to be a fellow cast member, her Victorian-era dress accentuating her beauty, but he soon realizes that, not only has he never seen her before, the dress isn't right for the production. Another look and she is gone... replaced by an older gentleman who quickly fades from view... followed by the giggling of a young boy. Far from being frightened, he is relieved. Seeing them is a good omen, a sure sign of a good show.

Theaters have always had a reputation of being haunted, as do churches. In the case of theaters, for one not to have a ghost is a sign of bad luck. Churches are founded on the promise of an afterlife, and usually those who enter them are quite faithful. Combining the two, it's easy to see why such a building would be considered haunted.

The History

Those who look at the Church Bistro & Theater usually find it deserving of its name. It does, after all, look less like a restaurant and dinner theater than it does an old church. The reason is that up until 1968, a church is what it was. Built in 1912, the building was for fifty-six years the home of the Alamo Methodist Church congregation. During that time, all manner of religious ceremonies occurred, from Sunday school to weddings, christenings, and funerals. It was, as churches often are, the hub of social activity and spiritual learning and growth for its members. In 1968, however, the congregation disbanded for unknown reasons. The members joined other congregations in the area, and the building sat empty for eight years.

In 1976, while driving in the area, Bill and Marcie Larson saw the building and immediately fell in love with it. They purchased the old church and began a massive renovation that included turning the lower level of Sunday school rooms into a restaurant and adding a stage to the upper-level sanctuary. They kept the pressed tin ceiling intact and were amazed to find the stained-glass windows unharmed. Their efforts earned them an award from the San Antonio Conservation Society.

In 1988, after much hard work, the building finally reopened as two separate entities, the Alamo Street Restaurant and the Alamo Street Theater. It was also given a spot on the National Register of Historic Places. Almost immediately after opening, there began to be whisperings of strange things going on in the building.

In 2005, the building was sold to Dr. Paul Alan Boskind, who combined the two businesses and renamed it the Church Bistro & Theater at King William.

The Ghosts...

According to the staff and guests, there are at least four resident specters that hang around—and maybe even more. In addition to the standard fare of cold spots, lights flickering, and unusual noises, there are also doors that open and close by themselves and instances of objects moving about unaided. Guests have caught photos of very strange things, including the mysterious lady in white, and the staff is happy to share the stories with anyone who asks. There is even a scrapbook containing all the encounters over the years.

Of the four main ghosts, the most famous is the woman in white, whom a psychic said was named Margaret. Miss Margaret, as the staff calls her, is always seen in a Victorian white dress, and most frequently is sighted around the stage area during performances. Those who have seen her have described her as looking remarkably like a woman named Margaret Gething, a local singer and actress who lived just a few streets away around the time the building was a church. The apparition began appearing one year after Miss Gething's death. Attached to Miss Margaret is another apparition, a woman who is believed to have been her seamstress, Henrietta; she is often seen near the stage and prop area.

Also present is the spirit of a little boy, who came to the theater apparently attached to a wheelchair bought secondhand as a prop. Though thought to have been confined to the chair in life, the boy no longer has any such limitations and has quite the reputation of being a prankster, particularly with the cooks. "Little Eddie," as he's called, has been known to move objects around and even has shoved one of the cooks into the refrigerator.

The fourth restless soul in the building has been long thought to be an actor from early in the theater's history. Alvin Martin was an actor in the Alamo Street Theater's production of "Born Yesterday." After much rehearsing, on opening night, Alvin said he wasn't feeling well, but the show had to go on. The next evening, he never arrived at the theater. When the stage manager went around to his home, he found Martin nearly comatose and rushed him to the hospital, where he died a few short days later. Since then, the tall man in a suit has appeared all over the building, often after late rehearsals, and has been reported waving to people from the bell tower.

Present Day

Today, the Church Bistro & Theater is a thriving business, offering daily lunch buffets and performances of plays year round. It is often used for weddings and receptions, and every year there is a special Halloween show that talks about the resident spirits. As for the ghosts, the employees and actors accept them as a part of the building and it's not at all uncommon to hear one of the cooks shouting for *Little Eddie* to leave her alone so work can get done.

Most of the apparitions appear in the theater's backstage area and kitchen, though Alvin is most often sighted after late rehearsals. The best bet for an encounter is to attend one of the many performances, although many of the restaurant patrons have had encounters with Little Eddie as well. To contact the theater or for more information, call 210-271-7791 or visit their web site at http://www.churchbistroandtheater.com.

Cadillac Bar Restaurant

212 South Flores
San Antonio, TX 78204

Cadillac Bar

On a hot summer day in Texas, nothing is better than going from the sticky street into an air-conditioned pub and ordering a frosty beverage. Inside, visitors find a quirky location rife with history, walls built of rough-hewn limestone, and good music. In all, a good place to escape the summer heat and relax for a few minutes. But there are places in this bar where some just won't go alone. The banquet rooms are full, but the waiters cast a nervous eye over their shoulders...*waiting for some unseen entity to grace them with her presence.*

Very few places in the world escape change. Historic buildings begin their lives as one thing, but are often recommissioned into something else. That a few buildings survive largely intact is nothing short of a miracle. But buildings, like people, draw on their past experiences to determine their identities. For every thing a building has been, something is left behind. It may be a mark in the rock or an additional room, or it might be something else that lives within – *the spirit of the building* – that people feel.

The History

German immigrant Herman Dietrich Stumberg and his son, George, originally built what is now known as the Cadillac Bar Restaurant in 1870. Made of heavy limestone, the building was first used as a general store that attracted business for miles and made the owners quite wealthy. During the 1880s, it has been theorized that, in addition to dry goods, the owners sold a different type of service—the kind that required them to employ young ladies. It's a theory that the previous owners vehemently deny and it remained the Stumberg General Store until around 1932.

Over the following years, the building was sold and used for a variety of businesses. One made saddles and other tack for cowboys. Another built boats. Still a third incarnation saw the old Stumberg building turned into a feed store.

In 1981, the Cadillac Bar Restaurant moved into the space. The bar, which was once operated as the Cadillac Bar in New Orleans, was moved out of the country during prohibition in favor of Mexico's more liberal views on alcohol. When it opened in San Antonio in 1981, it marked the first return of the Cadillac Bar to the United States since that time and 1984 saw the undertaking of a massive remodeling effort, earning an award from San Antonio's Conservation Society.

The Ghosts...

While most people are interested in spirits of a different sort, there are two of the restless variety that haunt the old building and a host of other interesting phenomena. From the sounds of crashing coming from the upstairs to heavy dragging noises, believed to be recurring from the time the building was a saddle company, the phenomena occur frequently. There are also instances of cold spots and whispers, though what the voices are saying can never be made out.

The first apparition that was seen in the building has been described as a tall thin man with a white handlebar mustache. He doesn't really do much other than hang about, but his image appearing out of nowhere when the bar is supposed to be closed and empty is certainly cause for alarm. Identified as possibly the uncle of the original owner, George Stumberg, "Uncle Herman" has been sighted near the kitchen area.

The other apparition is more of a mystery. Appearing only in the upstairs area, this woman in white was given the name Beatrice by a psychic who visited the establishment. Some believe her to have been a prostitute while others dismiss that theory. Whoever she was, she appears to be quite unhappy in the afterlife, often described as scowling at those who see her in the upstairs window.

Present Day

The year 1991 was when the building came full circle, as George Stumberg, the great-great-grandson of the man who built the building, became a stockholder in the Cadillac Bar Restaurant. The year 1992 brought more notoriety when the *Guinness Book of World Records* recognized the world's largest cocktail – a 1,551-gallon margarita made at the Cadillac Bar Restaurant – as record breaking. Interesting achievements aside, it functions today as a full-service restaurant, with catering available, live music, and a full bar.

The owner, Jesse Medina, has lost many employees over his thirty-two years in the establishment due to the otherworldly visitors. He says the phenomenon occurs with such regularity that it doesn't even startle him anymore.

The best times to visit the Cadillac Bar Restaurant are on Friday and Saturday nights, according to the owner, although anytime a person needs a cool drink and a friendly atmosphere works just as well too. The noises most often occur at night after closing, while the apparitions seem to come and go as they please. The fellow with the handlebar mustache tends to stay near the kitchen, while Beatrice stays in the upstairs private party room. For more information, contact the Cadillac Bar Restaurant at 210- 223-3746.

The Web House Cafe & Bar

517 East Woodlawn Street
San Antonio, TX 78212

The food is cutting edge, modern, and chic. The establishment combines the best of modern technology with fine dining on fare from several countries. It seems like the kind of place made in the modern world, where relics of the past lay buried and sleeping. But here, things are not only of the modern world. When the televisions turn off and the computers have powered down, there is a different sort of electricity that lurks within the walls. Whether natural or not, one cannot argue that this place, like so many others, has a memory of its former life.

No matter where a person goes, he can be secure in the knowledge that there was something in that spot before he got there. Considering the life of a building, one might marvel at the number of times it has been reinvented. Much like cleaning off a discarded piece of tin and finding a fine piece of art, many buildings become more than their histories have provided. Still those histories cannot, and in some cases won't be, ignored. Wherever emotions ran high, wherever there was love for a place, something lingers. Sometimes, *it* simply can't leave its home.

The History

Prior to its current incarnation, the building now called the Web House Cafe and Bar was a private residence. By most accounts and records, it remained in the hands of various private families until the 1980s, when a couple purchased the house and named it "Cafe Camille." It was during this time that strange things began happening in the home, giving birth to its haunted legend. Doors opened and closed seemingly at random and items were taken from off walls and moved to other locations by unseen hands. A visit from a psychic named the presence as the wife of a former owner who had died in the house many years before—and who was so attached that she just couldn't leave. It remained "Cafe Camille" as late as 1997, when Docia Shultz Williams' ran a short article on the disturbances there in her book *When Darkness Falls*. Between the publication of that book and 2007, however, Cafe Camille ceased operations.

There were a few references to the building in newspaper articles over the next nine years, with the exception of truncated versions of Ms. Williams' story. Then, in 2006, a young Russian immigrant purchased the former cafe. It was reborn under the name "Web House Cafe and Bar," boasting Internet access and cable television for its patrons, along with good food and a good atmosphere. Strange phenomena continued, though some, such as the floor in the main dining area spontaneously bursting into flame, were easily explained as a gas leak and quickly repaired. Still, not all within the house is at peace....

The Ghosts...

Mishka, the owner, knows the stories attached to the building, and while he has personally not experienced much in the way of the paranormal, he doesn't doubt the cafe's haunted reputation. While he and his employees do not feel that the presence is threatening, he does admit that there have been some unsettling things going on.

The most common phenomenon felt by the staff is the unshakable feeling of being watched. As if they are being followed, the employees know that wherever they go inside the Web House...they are never alone. Some customers have mentioned feeling that sensation as well.

The most overt phenomenon centers in the bar area, where the owner says he's come in on several occasions to find that the bar, a large, heavy wooden structure, has been moved eight or nine inches from its original place during the night. Though he has tried several methods, neither he nor anyone else can find a rational explanation for the seemingly supernatural relocation.

Present Day

Opened just a little more than a year (at the time of this book's publication), the Web House is still growing as a cafe and bar. Its menu continues to expand, as do its services. One constant, however, is the presence that is still felt within its walls. Whether it can be determined to be a true haunting down the road or not, the stories of the moving bar and phantom presences certainly do lend the place a bit of character.

The cafe also offers nightly events and catering. Ghosts not included.

The bar, it seems, only moves around after-hours, when the cafe is locked and the building is empty. The presences, however, occur throughout the year at random times. As the Web House Cafe and Bar serves breakfast, lunch, and dinner, has a happy hour, and hosts nightly events, perhaps the best strategy for staking out the location is to simply go and enjoy the food and the atmosphere. For more information, call 210-320-4280 or visit the cafe's web site at http://www.webhousecafe.com.

2

Haunted Hotels

To truly experience the culture and history of a city, especially one as old as San Antonio, many visitors choose to eschew the nameless, faceless chain hotels for something with a little more style. While the amenities at the other hotels may be quite luxurious, there simply is nothing quite like the feeling of a one-of-a-kind grand dame of the city. From the impressive architecture to the antique decor, staying at one of these hotels is like stepping back in time, your comfort catered by staff who care for not only the guests, but for the hotel itself. Walking through the halls, one is reminded of the old saying, *if only these walls could talk.* In some instances, however, they do.

The Menger Hotel

204 Alamo Plaza
San Antonio, TX 78205

The Menger Hotel

It's late at night and happy, but tired, guests carry their parcels to their rooms, their conversations abuzz with all they've seen that day. As they bid each other good night and step into their rooms, some catch a strange feeling. Perhaps a dark shadow darted just out of site, or maybe the outline of someone sitting on the bed is a trick of tired eyes. Why do some guests hear a child giggle in the hallways, and who is the odd woman in blue who dances through the old part of the hotel? Where did the maid go, the smiling woman with a scarf wrapped round her head? After speaking to the staff, it's little wonder that the grand Menger Hotel has the reputation of being the most haunted hotel in Texas.

Walking through the historic Alamo Plaza, visitors have a great deal to take in. Apart from the obvious monuments and the great old mission, there are more distractions than can easily be ignored. From attractions located prominently across the way to the Rivercenter Mall, it seems a fun place to while away the hours, looking at oddities courtesy of Mr. Ripley or picking through one of the many Texana tourist shops. But parked squarely in the middle of all the mayhem sits a stately old building, her windows rising high above the city streets as if watching over those who pass by. She has seen all but the very beginning of San Antonio, and her history is *alive* within her walls.

The History

Even after the bloody battle of the Alamo in 1836, San Antonio continued to flourish. Immigrants from Germany joined residents from Mexico in the prospering town, creating an economy that cried out for bigger and better things. Larger restaurants, finer shops, and more homes began to appear, drawing visitors from far and wide. William Menger, who was already a successful businessman through his tavern and beer brewery, decided to capitalize on the need and built what came to be known as the finest hotel in the state.

So fine the hotel was that it attracted not only regular tourists, but people whose fame preceded them. Captain Richard King of Texas' famous King Ranch kept a room in the Menger, as did famous writers O. Henry, Oscar Wilde, and Sidney Lanier. Actors and actresses such as Sarah Bernhard and Lillie Langtree, as well as Roy Rogers and Dale Evans, called the Menger home for a time. Royalty, senators, and even eleven Presidents have roamed the historic hallways, including Teddy Rosevelt, who recruited his "Rough Riders" over many a pitcher of Menger's beer in the bar, figuring hearty Texans would need less training at riding and shooting than men from other states.

However, as with any hotel the age of the Menger, life was not always parties and fame. There were times of strange incidents and others of real tragedy that befell the great lady. One of the stranger incidents that came to be something of a trademark for the hotel for a time occurred in the early 1900s when a fair performer skipped out on paying for his room. He did, however, leave his traveling companion: a 750-pound bull alligator, whom the staff took to calling "Bill." Bill lived happily in the atrium for some time and was even joined by other alligators.

In March 1876, tragedy struck the Menger when Sallie White, a long-time and well liked chamber maid, was shot three times by her jealous-crazed husband, who thought the worst of his wife working in a hotel. He was arrested on March 28, the day of the shooting, but because she didn't die straight away, he was released. He left town, never to return. Two days later, Sallie White passed away from her injuries. The hotel decided to cover her funeral costs, paying twenty-five dollars for her coffin and seven for her grave out of its own coffers. The entry of the monies paid out can still be seen in a display in the Menger's lobby.

The Ghosts...

There can be little doubt as to the validity of the Menger's unofficial title of "**Most Haunted Hotel**" in Texas. Speaking with long-time employee Ernesto Malacara, who has taken note of every strange phenomenon reported by guests and other employees, will turn a listener into a child around a campfire, with rapt attention paid to the stories he relates. Though the incidents number in the thousands, there appears to be less than fifty restless spirits that occasionally appear in the hotel. While most of their identities are unknown, a few are well recognized.

The most famous, and most often sighted, of apparitions is that of Sallie White, who continues to walk the halls of her beloved hotel. Always beautiful and wearing a white scarf around her head, she was at first only sighted in the older section of the hotel, but now has been reported in nearly every corridor. She's most often seen in the ballroom and kitchen, though she has been known to knock on the doors of guest rooms.

Other fairly consistent apparitions are those believed to be recruits of Roosevelt's "Rough Riders" in the bar. According to one unfortunate employee, he was cleaning the bar one night after closing and, after locking the door behind himself, turned to see a man in an old military uniform sitting at the bar, watching him. To make matters worse, the specter pointed at the young janitor and beckoned him with his finger. Panic-stricken, the young man forgot about having locked the door, and proceeded to bang on the door, shouting, until security came to get him. He refused to work in the hotel again.

There are also at least two "Ladies in Blue" that roam the halls of the hotel, one of whom seems to escape the walls to go dancing on the high ramparts of the neighboring Alamo. The other, who is described as a middle-aged woman wearing a blue dress with red embroidered stars on it and rather mannish boots, sits quietly in the original lobby, knitting or reading, until she is approached... then she promptly disappears.

Other restless souls at the hotel include a mischievous entity, called "Frisky" by employees, as he enjoys touching red-haired women; a little girl of about four years old who seems to have taken quite a liking to Richard, the night room-service waiter; a Spaniard; several Confederate soldiers; a man in buckskin; and Captain Richard King himself. There have been countless other phenomena, including strange rapping noises, reported bed levitations, people reporting faces other than their own staring at them from mirrors or from outside windows without balconies, and even tragic ghosts who committed suicide who replay the last moments of their lives before startled onlookers. Doors swing open without hands to push them, glasses sway without a hint of a breeze, and occasionally cigar smoke is smelled in non-smoking rooms. Countless other phenomena have occurred, corroborated not only by hotel staff, but also guests who say the paranormal pranks add an element of fun to their stay.

Present Day

The Menger Hotel has grown a bit over the years, and has changed hands several times. After the death of William Menger, it passed into the hands of the Kampmann family, and then to the Moody Family in 1943. It was awarded a state historic marker in 1980, and was named an historic hotel by the National Trust for Historic Preservation in 1989. Still a place of celebration, the Menger hosts an annual Halloween party for children, where Ernesto Malacara delights in retelling the haunted tales of his beloved hotel. It's also host to an annual Christmas party for underprivileged children, as well as other galas throughout the year. Most impressive is the fact that, for the Christmas and Halloween parties, the Menger charges nothing to the children.

As for the haunted activity, the Menger has become world famous. Activity there continues on a regular basis, prompting one employee to remark that not even a single week goes by without some new report coming in.

However, there is no "best time" for viewing these paranormal occurrences in the Menger Hotel, as the ghosts seem to keep to their own schedules. No particular time of year has ever proven to be more active than others, but there are specific places where people have had more activity. By far, most sightings occur in the older section of the hotel. Rooms on the second, third, and fourth floors have all had strange occurrences in them, though the staff won't say which rooms. One room that they will talk about is the room haunted by the restless spirit of Captain Richard King—the King suite. One reason may be that those who sleep in the King suite are sleeping in King's own bed, in which he died.

Another famously haunted area is the bar. Dark and beautiful, employees most often report guests that just seem to not want to leave right around closing time. Those same "guests" are often the ones who simply disappear before startled eyes.

For those who are interested in the ghosts of the hotel, Ernesto Malacara is the man to see. However, as one might imagine in a hotel the size of the Menger, his duties make him a very busy man. The easiest way to talk to him is to make an appointment. The toll free Reservation phone number is 800-345-9285. For more information, you can also go to the Menger's web site at http://www.historicmenger.com.

The Crockett Hotel

320 Bonham Street
San Antonio, TX 78205

The Crockett Hotel. *Courtesy of Bradford and Jennifer Johnson.*

hen one thinks about any given location, it's difficult not to see the here and now. Certainly, looking to the future is easily done, reliving past memories is common, but seeing a location before it even existed is hard to do. Before there were walls, a floor, or even a foundation, there was the land itself, and while it is far more common to talk about buildings that contain restless spirits, the land itself never forgets its history.

In historic hotels, it is not at all uncommon for stories of paranormal disturbances to be told. Tales of apparitions, whispered voices, and moving furniture are, it seems, part of hotel life, particularly if the hotel in question is more than one hundred years old. However, in some cases, the guests aren't the ones telling the stories. Instead of sleep interrupted by phantoms and apparitions being seen in the closets, it's the management that has encounters in, of all places, their offices.

The History

Though the building itself was erected in 1907, the history of the Crockett Hotel actually begins with the farmland on which it stands. While nothing but crops or cows roamed the land for years, its history took a decidedly macabre turn as it became part of the battlefield washed in the blood of soldiers during the Battle of the Alamo. It wasn't until 1874 that a French-born immigrant named Augustese Grenet purchased the land and opened a general store on the location. The store prospered, spurred on by the growing economy of the Republic of Texas.

Over the next thirty years, the property sold several times and took many forms. While, in some cases, it continued to function as a general store, in others it became a tavern. All that changed, however, in 1907, when San Antonio's arm of the International Order of Odd Fellows purchased the land with a grand plan. The existing building was torn down to make way for a combination lodge and hotel, owned and operated by the fraternity. It opened its doors for business in 1909, using the bottom four floors as luxurious hotel space and dedicating the top two floors to the Order. For more than seventy years, the hotel stayed in the possession of the Order, though the building began a steady slip into disrepair.

In 1978, the Order sold the building to an investor from Canada, who held it for only four years before the cost of upkeep and renovation forced another sale. This time, however, it was bought by John Blocker and his wife, Jenne, whose sister was involved with San Antonio's Historic Preservation Society. It took many years and painstaking work and research, but the Blockers managed to restore the old hotel, earning it a spot on the National Register of Historic Places.

The Ghosts...

As with any hotel as old as the Crockett, there are always stories. Former employees tell of things that happened late at night and guests may have an odd encounter of their own. The most commonly sighted apparition appears not in the guest rooms, but in the executive offices. He is a man in a dark blue jacket who is most commonly seen walking out the door toward the patio area, which used to be a Tavern.

Other reported phenomena include the presence of whispering voices, their conversations indecipherable, and curtains that move despite the absence of a draft and doors that open for no reason.

Present Day

The Crockett Hotel today is, along with the neighboring Menger Hotel, owned by 1859 Historic Hotels, or, more specifically, the Moody Family of Galveston. Truly keeping in its reputation and legacy for luxury, the hotel offers modern amenities with old-world charm. It also offers special package deals to fit with most travelers' schedules.

As for the restless spirits in the Crockett, they seem mostly quiet, with only a few sightings in recent years. Like with many hauntings, there appears to be no "best" time. The man in the dark jacket appears at random, always following the same path to a bar that no longer exists. Other phenomena happen infrequently. There have been no phenomena reported in guest rooms, as the executive offices seem to be the center of activity both for hotel operations and *otherworldly* visitors.

The toll-free Reservation line at the Crockett is 800-292-1050. For more information, visit its web site at http://crocketthotel.com.

The Gunter Hotel

205 East Houston Street
San Antonio, TX 78205

The Gunter Hotel. *Courtesy of Bradford and Jennifer Johnson.*

A man and a woman check in, but only he checks out, leaving behind a room soaked in blood and more questions than can easily be answered. It may sound like the setting for a "murder mystery weekend," but this mystery is real, and one of the most bizarre cases in San Antonio history. Why, then, if it is not an act, do some claim to still see the heinous crime? And who, if not actresses, are the period-dressed women who bicker in the hallway before disappearing in front of startled guests?

Many hotels have seen tragedy, but few can claim a legitimate mystery in their halls. Where the Gunter Hotel is concerned, events that have occurred in its rooms have inexorably made the stately hotel a part of not only history, but also of San Antonio folklore. Her guests today may be able to count on fine attention, but they might also catch a glimpse of the past...as history replays itself before their eyes.

The History

Since 1837, something has existed where now stands the Gunter Hotel. The original "Frontier Inn" was torn down in 1846 by an Irishman named Vance and his brothers to make way for a much larger building at the behest of the Confederate Army. The Vance building was used as the headquarters for the Confederates for a time, housing soldiers and officers, until the United States Military reclaimed it. In 1882, travelers again knew it for its amenities, as it was purchased by Ludwig Mahncke and Lesher Trexler, who renovated the property into what became known as the Mahncke Hotel.

In the 1900s, the lot was purchased by the San Antonio Hotel Group, which consisted of more than a dozen investors, including Lot Gunter. The old Mahncke Hotel was torn down to make way for what was to be known as an awe-inspiring structure. Designed by the same firm that created such titanic hotels as the Galvez in Galveston and the Adolphus in Dallas, the hotel boasted eight stories, more than three hundred rooms, and every modern amenity imaginable. It was named for Gunter, who had been the primary backer in the purchase, but who died before ever getting to see his namesake completed. It opened its doors on November 20, 1902 to rave reviews.

Construction continued in 1917 with the addition of a ninth story, and then three more in 1926, including a rooftop garden that became a hotspot for social events. The hotel became known as the center of social interaction, hosting parties of celebrities and dignitaries alike through the Roaring 1920s up until the 1960s. However, even with such a glorious history, there was bound to be some tragedy.

In February 1965, there occurred at the Gunter one of the most bizarre, and still unsolved, crimes in San Antonio's colorful history. A man checked into a room at the hotel under an assumed name with a thin blonde woman. Though they were seen over the course of several days, it wasn't until February 6 that a chambermaid happened upon a gruesome scene. As she opened the door, she saw the bed awashed with blood. The man who had checked in was clutching a large crimson-soaked parcel, but his female companion was nowhere to be seen. Without a word, the man dashed out the door and down the fire escape. Police later asserted that the amount of blood in the room indicated that someone had been murdered and butchered. The murderer was tracked to the St. Anthony hotel, where he had checked in under another assumed name. Before police could question him, however, he took his own life. The body of the woman was never found, nor was her identity learned.

Tragedy has not been the only thing to touch the Gunter, however. In its glorious history, it has played host to politicians, socialites, and celebrities. Stars Tom Mix and Mae West, philanthropist Will Rogers, and even former President Harry S. Truman stayed at the Gunter. John Wayne called the Gunter home while filming "The Alamo."

In 1979 the Gunter was sold to Josef Seiterle on behalf of a Swiss investment group that launched a $20 million refurbishing mission.

The Ghosts...

By far, the most famous ghosts in the magnificent hotel are a product of the unsolved crime of 1965—though they are not alone. In addition to the apparition of a woman in the tragic room, there have also been at least two others identified in the hotel. The first, called Ingrid, is most often seen in a long white dress on the upper floors. The second, nicknamed Peggy, has been identified as a 1920s-era flapper, who seemingly does not get along well with Ingrid. Though the two seem to stay on opposite ends of the hotel, there have been several odd occurrences attributed to the two of them fighting. Other occurrences include photos taken with extra people in them, moving furniture, and strange noises.

Present Day

In 1989, the Gunter became part of the world-famous Sheraton family hotel chain. Continuing its tradition of excellent attention to its guests and excellent amenities, the Gunter hosts weddings, banquets, and provides every service imaginable to ensure a great stay. As for the more spectral guests, there are still stories that pop up from time to time. While the ghost in the unsolved mystery room has been quiet for some time, the other permanent guests still appear, though more infrequently now.

At the request of hotel management, the room number in which the tragedy occurred will not be included here. However, what can be said is this: The room has since been renovated. While all the items in the room were, of course, removed soon after the tragedy, the room itself was divided years later into two smaller rooms. All that remains of the past is the tile floor in the bathroom. As for times, some say that the month of February is best for catching a glimpse of what happened so long ago, but the hotel management says they've never tracked the frequency of the reports. Suffice to say that, at the Gunter, it's best to just be observant.

For reservations, the Gunter's toll free line is 888-999-2089. More information can be learned on its web site at http://www.gunterhotel.com.

The St. Anthony Hotel

**300 East Travis Street
San Antonio, TX 78205**

The St. Anthony Hotel. *Courtesy of Bradford and Jennifer Johnson.*

There are places in the world where, once a person sees them, they are difficult to leave. Whether it's due to pleasant memories of times past, or feelings of luxury and being treated like royalty, or mingling with the upper crust, such places create a lasting impression on their patrons—*so much so that even in death, some return to relive their happy times*. It's for these reasons that some grand hotels seem to have guests who *never* leave and why there are reports of patrons in out-dated clothing that disappear when followed. And while the hotel staff regards their *otherworldly guests* with the same courtesy and love as the hotel itself, such phenomena give it the dubious distinction of being haunted.

As with people, some hotels must aspire to greatness while others are simply built great. Their high ceilings and decadent modern amenities shine like a beacon to royalty, who flock to mingle within its walls. The St. Anthony, named for the patron saint of the city itself, is just such a place. And while those who can only be described as royalty from the past and present may have called the hotel home for however brief a time, there are others who surely remember those bygone eras and will call her hallways home forever.

The History

The early 1900s in San Antonio was a time for prosperous growth for anyone with vision and enough brass to seize an opportunity. One such man was F. M. Swearingen, the former manager of the famed Hot Springs Resort Hotel of San Antonio. It was his desire to create a showplace hotel the likes of which the city had never seen. With the backing of a pair of cattle barons named B. L. Nayler and A. H. Jones, he set to work designing his palace. He purchased land belonging to Samuel B. Maverick for his site, demolishing the house on the lot and turning the orchard into present-day Travis Park. When it opened in 1909, throngs of the well-to-do lined up to get a glimpse at its modern amenities inside. Lighted closets, bedroom lights that turned off when the door was locked, and even private bathrooms were considered novelties of the time and gave the hotel its reputation as one of the most modern of the age, surely in the city.

In the first year alone, business was so good that a second tower was erected, and it was being favorably compared to the most famous of hotels in the nation. Customers flocked to rent rooms, despite its hefty (for the time) rates of $1.50 per night. Things seemed to be going well for the hotel until 1935, when the Great Depression crushed the American economy, and the hotel was put up for sale.

Against the counsel of his financial advisors, Ralph W. Morrison purchased the hotel and set about making costly improvements. Though times were bleak, Morrison was undeterred. His financial gamble paid off, however, resulting in hundreds more visitors wanting to sample the pampering and decadence the hotel provided. He added two stories to the top, combining the towers, and used the old elevator shafts as air conditioning ducts, creating the first central air-cooled hotel in the world. It continued to expand over the years until 1941 when the attack on Pearl Harbor brought more important things to mind than hotel expansion.

It was during this time that some of Hollywood's most influential and powerful people stayed at the St. Anthony, touting the use of war bonds. Meetings of not only Hollywood's powerful, but the world's most powerful people were held in the hotel's conference rooms. It took little time for the owner to see the rich and famous, the powerful and elite in one place before he created the St. Anthony Club, an elite social caste that featured fine dining, celebrity guests, and some of the hottest bands of the era. It's said that some of the most powerful and influential deals went down behind the locked doors of the St. Anthony's meeting rooms.

In 1965, the St. Anthony found its way into another section of San Antonio history for its unintended role in the bizarre mystery crime that also affected the Gunter Hotel. It was the St. Anthony to which the murder suspect fled, registered under an assumed name, and committed suicide in one of the rooms.

The Ghosts...

While many hotels boast restless spirits, few can match or beat the St. Anthony for the number of permanent guests it has.

And while most everyone agrees there is nothing in the hotel that will hurt anyone, some of the phenomena can be, at first, a little unsettling.

The staff has long spoken of something haunting the downstairs men's locker room. Though alone, some have heard the sounds of an employee washing up in an empty stall. Others talk of shadowy outlines, doors that open and close on their own and the sounds of footsteps that follow people down otherwise empty halls.

Often reported by both guests and employees are the apparitions of unknown individuals who simply seem to not wish to leave. There is a woman in red who is often seen wandering the halls—she is also often blamed for a pair of stocking-clad legs that appear beneath the door of the first stall of the women's restroom. She never comes out of the stall, though, and people have watched as her legs eventually just fade and vanish. There have also been reports of a tall man in a dark suit who rides the elevators and then disappears when he exits on the tenth floor. There have even been a few cases in which patrons insist their rooms are already occupied by a man and woman, both toasting and wearing evening wear. Investigation provides no trace of them. Neither has anyone been able to discover the identity of a man in a tuxedo or a woman in a white chambermaid's uniform who both routinely appear and disappear in the maid's station.

In addition, there are reports of televisions turning on and off in unoccupied rooms, locks that lock on their own, and slapping noises against doors in the middle of the night. While writing her book *When Darkness Falls*, Docia Williams had a strange encounter when her room suddenly filled with the scent of perfume, which then just as suddenly dissipated. Also, while researching the place, a member of her group was whistling in the stairwell and, when he stopped, someone who could not be seen whistled back.

Present Day

In 2001, the St. Anthony was purchased by Apollo Investments and became one of the Wyndham properties. As it did in the past, it caters to the royalty of the day. In the past, names such as Eleanor Roosevelt, General Douglas McArthur, Judy Garland, Mickey Rooney, Fred Astaire, and Lucille Ball held court in her hallways, as did Prince Rainier and Princess Grace of Monaco. Today, when modern demigods descend from the heavens, many choose to stay in the St. Anthony's loving embrace. Names like Arnold Schwarzenegger, Patrick Swayze, George Clooney, Demi Moore, and Bruce Willis can be found in the registry.

Of those names not found in the registry, however, there are still tales. And while no one is sure of their names, or their purposes, they are welcome in the hotel like any other guest.

The most active floor in the hotel seems to be the tenth, where the rooftop garden once hosted parties for the rich and famous. Though the gardens may be gone, the memories, it seems, linger. While most of the phenomena occur at random, there is one whispered time of year when one might catch a glimpse of the man who shot himself in connection with the unsolved crime of 1965. It's during the earliest week of February that there have been unconfirmed rumors that the tragic and gruesome scene replays.

For reservations, call 877-999-3223. Also visit its web site at http://www.wyndham.com/hotels/SATST/.

Bullis House Inn/International Hostel

**621 Pierce Street
P.O. Box 8059
San Antonio, TX 78208**

Bullis House Inn and International Hostel. *Courtesy of Bradford and Jennifer Johnson.*

While some travelers prefer the comfort and security of staying at a "name" hotel, choosing one out of hundreds that assure quality but may lack personality, others prefer the personal touch of home hospitality that only a Bed & Breakfast-style inn can provide. Instead of an ever-rotating staff, guests are treated like family, their needs tended to in a home and not just a room. Within the walls, however, there are sometimes guests who just refuse to give up their comfortable bed, or others who knew the home as something other than a restful place, and who still do not rest within the walls.

Finding a Bed & Breakfast is no difficult chore, nor is finding one with historic significance in San Antonio. Some places, however, have a more colorful history than others. Oftentimes, the original owner was so great a personality that his impression is left on the home he built. Other times, they are his deeds that linger on, a bubble in time. Whatever the case, a Bed & Breakfast is a different type of entity in that it always has two things in abundance: Hospitality—and *ghosts*.

The History

Brigadier General John Bullis was, by all accounts, a great man. His battles against Native Americans earned him the reputation of a fierce warrior, while his dealings with his own troops earned him respect and admiration. It was he who orchestrated the capture of Apache Chief Geronimo, and later became an Indian statesman. When he retired to San Antonio in the early 1900s, he had the rest of his life in mind. He built his new home, including in the plans an extra-wide front door to accommodate his coffin and pallbearers in the event of his passing. The design proved prophetic as in 1911, only two years after moving into his new home, General Bullis did indeed die.

After laying in state in the living room for a week, his pall-bearers made good use of the extra-wide front door. The house was left to the remaining members of the Bullis family, and for the next three decades, they owned and lived in the home. In 1949, the house was sold to another famous general, Jonathan Wainwright, who rented the place out as professional office space. At one point, the house was even rented as a childcare center.

By 1983, the home had fallen into disrepair. Age and upkeep were both on the high side, prompting the sale of the house again, this time to Steve and Alma Cross, who began a period of extensive renovations and transformed the home into the Bullis House Inn Bed & Breakfast. It was during these renovations that the first incidents began to occur, hinting that there may be *something* in the home left over from the previous occupants.

The Ghosts...

While most might think it would be the restless spirit of General Bullis himself who haunts the home, the most common apparition may actually be someone who is just looking for him. Identified as a young Apache Indian, the apparition has appeared to multiple people simultaneously, but has never threatened anyone.

Other phenomena began when the Crosses started renovating, beginning with the sounds of two men arguing in the downstairs area when the house was otherwise unoccupied and the doors were locked. A quick check of the property by Steve Cross revealed no intruders.

At least one guest, who verified the phenomena with the manager, tried to go up the back stairwell only to find his way blocked by an unseen force. Others have reported unlocked doors that will not open, as if someone were holding them in place from inside the room. These same guests leave to get the manager and return to find the door standing wide open.

Present Day

Still owned by the Crosses, the Bullis House Bed & Breakfast had historic markers placed in its backyard in 2005, commemorating the site where Belgian astronomer Jean-Charles Houzeau observed the planet Venus as it passed between the earth and the sun in 1882. It has been recommended by both the *New York Times* and *Southern Living* as a fantastic place to stay while in the city, and it still offers what the owners describe as "affordable elegance in the classic Southern style."

When asked about the paranormal aspects of the hotel, Alma Cross gives a knowing chuckle. "We've been featured in books and magazines before," she says, acknowledging the inn's place in San Antonio's supernatural hierarchy. While infrequent and never threatening, the restless souls of the Bullis House are part of what gives the place its personality.

The apparition of the Indian has appeared in both the upstairs and downstairs of the home, and seems to hold to no schedule. The voices, however, were clearly heard coming from the entry area of the downstairs, while it was the back stairway that guests found blocked by an unseen force. It seems that the best hope of experiencing anything paranormal is to check in and keep your eyes open. While there are certainly no guarantees, at the very least guests will get a wonderful night in an amazing piece of history.

For reservations, call 877-477-4100. Also visit its web site at http://www.bullishouseinn.com.

Columns on Alamo Bed & Breakfast

**1037 South Alamo Street
San Antonio, TX 78210**

The Columns on Alamo Bed and Breakfast

After a long day of seeing the sights, few things can be better than sleeping in one's own bed. For most visitors to the historic city, such accommodations are not possible. A wonderful second choice, which many find liking more than their own homes, is one of the beautiful Bed & Breakfast Inns. In these places, the rooms are beautifully decorated, the beds are soft, and the owners do their best to ensure the comfort of their guests. In some, however, the owners are not the only ones who check to make sure everything is alright. Though unseen but generally welcoming, such presences give the inn a different type of distinction: That of being haunted.

Not every haunting is caused by a horrific death or human suffering. In many cases, it's simply the presence of strong emotions that seem to be the culprit. Not only negative emotions, but also strong feelings of love, caring, and joy can leave impressions on places that held them, allowing those who experience them the privilege of their feelings, and turning what might otherwise be just another hotel or inn into a warm and loving home.

The History

What would become known as one of the best Bed & Breakfast-style inns in San Antonio actually dates back to 1869, when Thomas J. Devine owned the three lots on the corner. How or why he acquired them is unknown, but it is known that sixteen years later, he sold the lots to George Altgelt, who combined them to make two one-and-a-half lot parcels before building his home. He lived there for less than six years before the properties were sold again. His home went to a hardware merchant named Tipps while Mrs. Jacobine Eichmeyer purchased the undeveloped lot.

Although Eichmeyer had a home built on the site, she never lived there. It was rented less than two years when Edward Reuss, who owned the City Drug Store, purchased the property. Reuss lived there until his death and the house was sold again to Anton Heinen in 1911. Heinen is credited with expanding the structure and creating on it the recognizable columns and face it still wears today. He lived in the house for more than fifty years until his death in the 1960s. It was purchased by Amparo and Rudolph Leos, who lived in the home until 1993; that's when current owners Art and Eleanor Link found the place for sale. Since that year, the Links have put loving care into the home, turning it from an aging home into a world-class beauty.

The Ghosts...

Art Link chuckles when asked about the inn's otherworldly inhabitants. Though skeptical, he does admit to some strange goings on inside his hotel, specifically in one room. It's in that room that some guests have felt a strange presence, identified by one as a "negro nanny." It makes sense, as the room in question was once a nursery connected to the master bedroom.

On another occasion, a couple from Holland stayed at the inn and came to the front desk complaining that they could not get into their room. Mr. Link looked into the room from an outside window to see that the door's deadbolt had somehow turned itself. He wound up having to break down the door and make repairs later.

Present Day

The Links have turned the old home into a veritable showplace. A part of the King William Historic District, Columns on Alamo offers thirteen antique-furnished rooms, private baths, and an award-winning hearty breakfast. Although still skeptical, Art Link seems to take the reports of weird happenings in stride.

Most of the incidents seem to happen at night. The mysteriously locked door was discovered after a long day of taking in the sights and the perceived presences are felt just after the sun dips down. However, no one in the inn has ever felt threatened or frightened by whatever restless soul still walks the hallways. If it is indeed the nanny, most likely she, like the owners, are simply concerned with the comfort of the guests.

The toll free phone number for the inn is 800-233-3364. For more information, visit its web site at http://www.columnssanantonio.com.

Emily Morgan Hotel

705 East Houston Street
San Antonio, TX 78205

$\int$ he looms over the street, her high pointed tower and steeply angled walls making her appear much taller than she actually is. Gargoyles adorn her roof, doorways, and windows, giving the building the look and feel of a castle. Yet, for all her imposing might, the old hotel is a welcoming and warm place. Inside, the beds are turned down, the rooms are comfortable, and the view is unparalleled. There is also something else, however. Inside the walls, the past is alive, for she was not always a hotel. Her job, though radically different, is still to care for those in need, but today those people are there by choice.

Looking up from Houston Street, it's easy to be intimidated by the site of the Emily Morgan Hotel. Thirteen stories of stone and steel seem to cleave the skyline, cutting a swath through clouds and birds, commanding the respect she deserves. But looking up at the gargoyles that adorn her walls, one can't help but notice that some appear to be ill while others seem to suffer from other maladies. One even seems to have a toothache. Why would someone build such strange sculptures into the side of a hotel? And who exactly was Emily Morgan anyway? It's all part of the fascinating history and the mystery of the hotel that bears her name.

The History

As with most things that neighbor the famous Alamo landmark, the history of the Emily Morgan Hotel must begin with the ground on which she's built. Once awash with blood, the land saw more than its share of death and suffering. It

The Emily Morgan Hotel

stood vacant until 1926 when the massive gothic structure was built as the city's first Medial Arts Building. It was considered the first documented "skyscraper" west of the Mississippi. While much of the downstairs area was used for doctors' offices, the top several floors were used for an actual hospital with the basement of the building serving as the morgue. According to lore, the top floors were used for surgery so that windows could be opened and the smell would not permeate the whole building.

When the building ceased being a medical facility, it was first used as an office building; it was then sold again and rechristened The Emily Morgan Hotel.

Emily Morgan was the name mistakenly given to a beautiful Mulatto woman who seduced and distracted General Santa Anna, giving her employer, Colonel Morgan, time to attack. Most assumed her to be Morgan's slave and therefore gave her his last name. Actually, she was a free woman whose last name was West. Despite the confusion over her name, her role in Texas history remains the same. Because of her efforts, Morgan won. She was also, for a time, reputed to be the woman about whom the song "The Yellow Rose of Texas" was written, but that theory has since been proven false. Still, in the minds of many Texans, the song and the name conjures up visions of pure beauty. In the case of the Emily Morgan Hotel, the description fits.

The year 1997 saw a partial renovation, followed by a multi-million dollar complete makeover from 2001 to 2002. With 177 rooms and twenty-four suites, the Emily Morgan has the well-deserved reputation of remarkable service and elegance.

The Ghosts...

There can be no doubt as to the reason behind the haunting of the former battleground and hospital. The hotel has been featured several times on television and in books and magazines.

Among the more innocuous phenomena reported are doors that open and close by themselves and objects that tend to move unaided by any visible means. Docia Schultz-Williams interviewed a guest who spoke about seeing a bottle and a coffeepot scoot across the counter before smashing to the floor. That same guest experienced a loud slamming of the toilet in her room that went on for nearly an hour. Add to that the occasional temperamental elevator and odd smell—and there's enough to give anyone pause.

Of course, the most interesting and startling phenomena come from the apparitions that occasionally dash through rooms, passing through solid walls or appearing in mirrors. Several guests tell tales of a man that simply passes through without so much as a wave, an echo replaying a moment from his life. As to the ones that appear in mirrors, they have never hurt anyone, but appear as if they are simply checking in from time to time.

Present Day

The year 2002 saw the grand re-opening of the hotel with a massive golden-themed bash, along with the opening of the hotel's new restaurant, "Oro." Though fully modernized, there are still little signs of the hotel's past. The fact that the elevator has no button for the thirteenth floor, but does for a fourteenth floor, hearkens back to hotel superstition that to have thirteen floors is unlucky. Still present on the walls are gargoyles left from the building's hospital days. Looking closely, one can see that each of the sculptures suffers from some form of malady that the hospital treated. Also still visible is the blank face between the "fourteenth" floor and the observation tower, where an intended clock was never installed.

Still, strange things do happen in the hotel, but far from being alarmed, most guests take the hotel's spirits in stride.

As there seems to be no malevolent entities at the hotel, guests who stay in the luxurious rooms are indeed able to rest peacefully.

Most of the disturbances in the hotel are centered on floors seven, eight, nine, fourteen, and the basement. It was on the "fourteenth" floor that most of the gruesome surgery took place, and the basement, which was used as the morgue, is now accessed by employees only.

For more information, call 212-255-5100 or visit the hotel's web site at http://www.emilymorganhotel.com.

Inn on the Riverwalk

129 Woodward Place
San Antonio, TX 78204

The Inn on the Riverwalk. *Courtesy of Bradford and Jennifer Johnson.*

The waters of the Riverwalk run past the old houses, its current silent but for a whispering babble against the concrete banks. Too far down to hear the cries of the boat captains or the revelries of the bars, this spot is quiet and serene, just close enough to enjoy the benefits with a quick walk, but far enough away for a restful night's sleep. But could it be that, even here, the drumbeat from the restaurants can be felt, that the revelers can be heard? And why is it that, in certain areas, one has the distinct impression of not being alone? There is no explanation, no source, and no cure. There are only the experiences that leave most intrigued, and others charmed.

Not every place with haunted activity was the site of a bloody battle, a heinous murder, or even a jealous lover's spat. In some cases, that which lingers in the house defies identification, its origin unknown. Research going back to before the home was built might show nothing more than happy families and farmland, but something still lurks. Whether a restless spirit, misplaced soul, or something else, those who experience its effects have little doubt in their minds that, whatever else the house is or may have been, it's also haunted.

The History

What makes the Inn on the Riverwalk so remarkable is that, in a field where tragedy and suffering make up a majority of stories, its history is so unremarkable. There appear to have been no tragedies, no suicides, and no quarreling lovers resulting in a violent death. In fact, there seems to be nothing remarkable about the history of the hotel whatsoever.

Built in 1916, the silver-roofed Victorian-style mansion was, in fact, a home. Built by whom and for what purpose are footnotes apparently lost to time, but for forty-three years the building seemed to function as a simple home. While it has been noted that several families lived in the home prior to the 1950s, all those who dwelled within had happy, normal lives. In 1959, this old house had its insides rearranged and was turned into apartments. It remained that way for fifteen years; that's when Dr. Arthur Zucht purchased the building in 1974.

Although the house was purchased in what he called "good condition," he set to work restoring it to the home he felt it was meant to be. After some renovations the building was opened up and reborn as the Inn on the Riverwalk. Dr. Zucht is the first to report any type of paranormal activity in the house, though he felt the presence was a kind one, and did not let it bother him or his guests. In May of 2007, Dr. Zucht sold the inn to new owners, but stayed on for a while to help transition the change.

The Ghosts...

While the new owners are not certain, Dr. Zucht is quite sure. He believes the place to be genuinely haunted, though he feels the specter is a positive entity. On several occasions, he witnessed beds vibrating and heard loud noises coming from above, as if from the above room. However, further investigation revealed the room above to be vacant. He also stated that there were several times when he felt a presence, though it was by no means harmful.

Present Day...

With sixteen guest rooms spread out in three buildings, the Inn on the Riverwalk has been updated from a group of 1916-era homes to a model of modern comfort. All the rooms are tastefully decorated, promising a relaxed and restful stay. The inn also offers wedding and reception services, as well as event accommodations, both corporate and private.

Only time will tell if the haunted activity at the inn continues. Although the present owners appear somewhat skeptical, they seem willing to give the place the benefit of the doubt.

Most of the phenomena seems to occur at night, and only in two rooms, though which two rooms were not named. The best time, therefore, seems to be when one is in need of a restful romantic weekend away.

For more information about the Inn on the Riverwalk, call 210-225-6333 or visit its web site at http://www.innonriver.com.

Ogé House Bed & Breakfast

209 Washington Street
San Antonio, TX 78204

Oge House. *Courtesy of Bradford and Jennifer Johnson.*

In the kitchen, something's cooking. The rich aroma fills the air, teasing the nostrils and tempting the palate. Just a few things more added, and the dish will be perfect. A pinch of this and a smidgeon of that are placed in the bowl, but something is wrong. A stiff breeze has sprung up from nowhere, indoors, and without the benefit of an air conditioning vent to convey it. A quick puff and spices are thrown about the kitchen, leaving the bewildered chef to wonder if he should have chosen the paprika instead. As the old saying goes, too many chefs spoil the soup, but that only holds true if both the chefs are, in fact, alive.

Historic homes always have a story or two to tell. Whether influenced by paranormal energies or not, they all have their quirks, whether in the form of a slanted floor or a window that just won't stay closed for some reason. In some cases, however, the phenomena goes beyond mere household peculiarities. There sometimes comes the question of just who owns the house, the living or the dead.

The History

While the exact date of construction of the Ogé house is unknown, it is certain that between the years 1857 and 1860, a San Antonio attorney named Newton Mitchell and his wife, Catherine Elder Mitchell, had the house built. They were not long to live in their new home, however, as Mrs. Mitchell passed away in 1862, followed only two years later by her husband. The house passed into the hands of Catherine's sister, who rented it out for several years. In 1868, the home was sold to a woman named Eudora Abrahams, but sold again only two years later to another woman named Catherine Sampson.

Sampson lived in the house for eleven years until selling it in 1881 to a former Texas Ranger and cattle-baron named Louis Ogé (pronounced oh-jhay). Ogé was a man of singular experience, having been a Texas Ranger at the young age of eighteen and then moving on to more lucrative opportunities. By the time he was twenty-eight, he'd started ranching for a living. His ranch was so prosperous that he retired in 1881 with his wife, Elizabeth, and four children, Josephene, George, Annie, and Frank.

When Louis Ogé died in 1915, his wife continued residence in the home. She stayed until 1942, when the house was sold and turned into apartments. A succession of owners followed until 1991, when it was purchased by Pat and Sharrie Matatagen, who went to work restoring the place. As soon as construction began, Sharrie Matatagen began to feel and see things that she could only explain as a haunting.

The Ghosts...

There are several entities that seem attached to the Ogé house. Though none have been identified by name, there are three whose presences have been felt on several occasions. The impression of a man follows the feeling of a woman throughout the house. The woman may in fact be Mrs. Ogé, but the man still defies identification. There also lurks the presence of a ten-year-old child whom psychics believe drowned in the river, on the banks of which the house sits. Most consider the presences in the house to be benevolent and welcoming, but on at least one occasion, one of them (presumed to be Mrs. Ogé) disagreed with the types of spices being used in the dinner. She proceeded to blow the spices out of the pot and all over the kitchen. Other phenomena include lights going on and off and cold spots.

Present Day

Recently, the Ogé house was sold to Liesl and Don Noble of Noble Inns, LLC. Still keeping in the same tradition, several rooms have been remodeled to enhance the luxurious feel of the inn. It joins the Jackson House and the Carriage House in the King William Historic District as inns that add a touch of class and history to any stay.

As construction and remodeling continues, it's believed that the paranormal activity will increase. The home, according to the previous owners, was fairly quiet for some time after renovation was complete, but with new renovations, the phenomena could continue.

While the supernatural happenings appear to be scattered throughout the inn, there seems to be two areas of concentrated activity. The Mathis room has been the focal point of several disturbances, incidents of lights flashing on and off and a few random noises, while the kitchen seems to be another focal point. The area of the present-day kitchen, it should be noted, was once the bedroom of Mrs. Ogé.

The toll-free number of the Ogé is 800-242-2770. Also visit its web site, http://www.nobleinns.com, for more information.

3

Haunted Missions

Certain types of places lend themselves to being haunted. Haunted houses from which families flee in terror are the most famous, but any place where emotions run high, where faith is tested, and where people suffer either physical or emotional stress is a fertile candidate for a haunting. For that reason, many paranormal investigators target hospitals, battlefields, and even airports for scrutiny. One type of place commonly found to have permanent visitors is that which many associate with spirits anyway: churches.

In San Antonio, before the land was tamed and before there were churches of every conceivable religion, there were those who brought religion to the land. Franciscan monks came from Spain, building missions along the way. Far from being only churches, the missions were, in fact, tiny cities that mirrored the way of life of Spain. In some cases, the Native Americans didn't want to be converted and the missions became the sites of bloody conflict. Small wonder, then, that the adobe brick and stonewalls sometimes whisper with their own stories. There were five missions built by the Spanish in San Antonio, all of them along the winding river. Because of their very nature, and because of revolution, all five seem to have residents who simply will not leave.

The Alamo

300 Alamo Plaza
P.O. Box 2599
San Antonio, TX 78299

The Alamo

uests file past the heavy wooden doors to see the inside of the great old church. Although this is a popular tourist spot, no one here is loud or boisterous. Many stand with their heads bowed in reverence, their hands clasped before them. There is a sense of melancholy here, a sense of determined pride. Even children can feel the *building breathing*...and hear the walls weeping for those who died inside. Glancing at the plaques on the walls reveals legends with names like Travis, Bowie, and Crockett, and while it's obvious that something awful happened on these grounds, it's also apparent that, without that sacrifice, the great state of Texas wouldn't even exist today.

Battlegrounds are notorious for paranormal activity. Places like Gettysburg and Wounded Knee, where thousands died in agony for what they believed, have long since held a sort of holy reverence for those who visit them. Although the history of Texas is filled with one bloody battle after another, there is none so famous as the one that took place in a tiny mission in San Antonio. Those who died in defense of the state still whisper, their sacrifices mourned, by a grateful people who will always *remember* the Alamo.

The History

Originally called the Mission San Antonio de Valero, Franciscan monks built the structure now known as The Alamo as a place where they could teach Native Americans about their religion. The site was chosen after the disastrous failure of another mission near present-day Nacogdoches, which resulted in the monks fleeing for their lives. Under a cottonwood tree, the monks decided that this would be a much more suitable location from which to spread their philosophy. Built in 1718, the church met with greater success and San Antonio as a city began to flourish. For nearly eighty years, the mission continued operations, prompting the construction of four other missions in the city. Then, in 1793, Spain began secularizing their missions, beginning with San Antonio de Valero. The mission became known more as a fort, and was given a nickname by which it was known because of the cottonwood tree sitting outside its gates. "Alamo," as it became known, was Spanish for "cottonwood."

By January of 1836, the old mission had become a repository for armaments won in battle. General Sam Houston, not wanting the armaments to fall into the hands of Santa Anna, ordered Colonel James Bowie, the volunteer soldier for whom the giant double-edged knife was named, to go to the old mission with the purpose of demolishing it. He was to line the walls with dynamite and gunpowder and blow the building apart until nothing was left. Bowie, however, realized that the mission was the last line of defense between the forces of Mexico's dictator and the burgeoning Texas Republic. With word of Santa Anna's army marching across Mexico and into Texas, he knew the old mission would be a key point in defense. He also realized that moving more than two-dozen cannons without the benefit of carts or oxen, only with his regiment of twenty-five men, would be close to impossible. Instead, he set to work reinforcing the structure as a stronghold.

Shortly thereafter, Colonel William Travis arrived, bringing his garrison of more than one hundred men with him. When Santa Anna's army arrived in Texas earlier than planned, he sent frantic messages to the governments in Texas begging for supplies and reinforcements. No one replied.

On February 19, a group of twenty volunteers, led by statesman and legend David Crockett, were chased into town by Mexican forces. They took refuge in the old church and agreed to fight alongside the volunteer forces and the regular army soldiers. Travis sent more pleas for help, stating that they would either be victorious or die in the effort. He also stated that, if the Texas government did not send aid, his dead bones would forever reproach his country for its neglect. Four days later, Santa Anna reclaimed San Antonio and raised the red flag that signaled no quarter would be given. He sent his demand for the surrender of the Alamo, which, legend has it, the Texans answered with a cannon blast.

The last, and only, reinforcements to answer Travis' pleas for help were a group of about fifty men from Gonzalez. Three days later, Santa Anna's forces began their final assault. What happened inside the walls that day became the stuff that legends are made of. Many details are based on hearsay, as every Texan combatant died in the fight. Travis was among the first to die, wading into the battle with his rifle erupting thunder. Crockett has been forever immortalized in image as standing fighting hand to hand, swinging his musket rifle "Betsy" over his head like a club when he ran out of bullets. Bowie, who was struck down with typhoid-pneumonia before the battle began, is said to have shot several from his bed before being overcome and stabbed to death with bayonets. Whether completely true or not, the images of the Texas heroes fighting to their final moments became the lasting image by which the Alamo was known, spreading the battle cry of "Remember the Alamo" through the rest of the nation. At the end of the day, all 189 defenders lay dead, more than 1,500 Mexican soldiers perished, and more than five hundred Mexican soldiers were wounded. Though Santa Anna claimed a victory, one of his own soldiers stated that another such victory would destroy Mexico.

Santa Anna denied the fallen soldiers burials, commanding instead that the bodies be stacked and burned in three pyres. The remains were later gathered and buried, but the location of the grave is still unknown. Although they died, the proud Texans of the Alamo provided time for the Texas government to organize for the battle of San Jacinto, allowing a victory and ensuring Texas' freedom.

The Ghosts...

Whether a person knows the gruesome details of the battle or not, anyone who enters the structure can feel the presence of those who died. So much pain and death is found in few places in the nation, but battlefields are famous for those who do not rest. From the placard outside that asks reverence for those who died to the displays inside, anyone who enters can feel the sacrifices made. There are several legends about the Alamo—and they're all related to supernatural occurrences.

The earliest mention of something paranormal came only days after the battle, when Santa Anna ordered the mission burned to the ground. He did not want the building to become a shrine to the fallen Texans who defied him. His field commander, General Andrade, sent a group of soldiers to complete the task. When they returned a short while later, all of them were shaken and refused to go back, claiming that six "devils" had appeared, all with flaming swords, to repel them. The General himself decided to burn it anyway, but after he too was repelled by the spectral images, he took his soldiers and left the mission intact.

In 1871, the city laid out plans to dismantle part of the old mission, leaving only the long barracks and the church. When the announcement was made, a curious rash of reports came from the neighboring Menger Hotel—patrons claimed to see a ghostly army marching the walls, as if defending it from destruction.

Since then, there have been numerous sightings and legends, which center around three specific phenomena. The first is the appearance of a spectral guard on the south side of the roof, always marching from east to west, on rainy or drizzly nights. The second comes from the numerous reports of an overwhelming feeling of sadness and heaviness in the main chapel area. Many who go in have been observed to burst into tears, often unaware of their doing so. The third phenomena is another apparition, that of a crazed man at the southwest corner of the mission. He is rumored to be guarding more than half a million dollars in twenty-dollar gold pieces buried at the location. Other phenomena reported include phantom footsteps, cold spots, and whispers when the building is otherwise empty.

As an interesting side-note, famed movie star John Wayne, while filming the movie "The Alamo," visited the site often. To him, it represented everything that he stood for: patriotism, freedom, and bravery. According to some, the actor's spirit occasionally returns to commune with the building and with the spirits of the soldiers who died there.

Present Day

Although it has served other purposes, the Alamo has always been a symbol of Texas freedom. In 1905, the Daughters of the Republic of Texas were granted custodianship over the old mission, and have maintained it ever since. Existing solely on donations, the DRT keep the Alamo open to the public without charging admission so that it will truly never be forgotten. Today, only the original long barrack and chapel remain of the original structure, with a gift shop and other exhibits added. The building is also the meeting place of several "Haunted San Antonio" walking tours. In addition, it has become the focal point of tourism in San Antonio, with several attractions springing up around it.

The phenomena continue, with sensitives (a person attuned to paranormal forces) and guests alike feeling the history of the building. The guards often tell stories about what goes on when no one else is around, and there seems to be no sign of it stopping any time soon.

The Alamo is open every day except Christmas Eve and Day, and is free to the public. Most of the phenomena occurs on the anniversary of the battle, in the month of March. However, the spectral guard reputedly walks on rainy nights, his vigil kept over the roof of the mission. For more information, visit the Alamo's web site at http://www.thealamo.org.

San José y Miguel de Aguayo

6701 San Jose Drive
San Antonio, TX 78214

Mission San José y Miguel de Aguayo. *Courtesy of Bradford and Jennifer Johnson.*

It has been called the Queen of the Missions, the finest example of a Spanish mission of its time. From the ornately carved windows to sculptures around the doors, it's a testament to human achievement and belief. Those who pass through her doors often talk of a sense of serenity, as if the worries of the world melt away, but there are other things here than just peace. For while the mission was built for the Glory of God, thousands died to ensure that the Queen was worthy of their Lord.

At more than two hundred years old, the Mission San José y Miguel de Aguayo has seen a great deal of Texas history. Its hardships and victories, births, weddings, and deaths all have happened within the crumbling stonewalls. For a building like this to have survived so many troubles and still be a place of worship proves that buildings don't make churches...people and love do. Some of those people, it seems, loved the building so much they couldn't leave it, even in death. And while such feelings are called holy, reverent, or sacred, there is another term for them: Haunted.

The History

Franciscan monks built the Mission San José y Miguel de Aguayo in 1720 along what is now known as the "mission trail." Its purpose was to spread the word of God by converting the Native Americans to Christianity. History shows that the proud natives did not immediately take to liking the missionaries, leading to several violent and bloody conflicts. The mission was moved in 1727, and again to its final resting spot in 1744. Within five years, the monks and Native Americans who lived within its walls had completed construction of the mission's grain mill and friary, as well as stone houses for the natives and the beginnings of an adobe church. The main sanctuary followed, with intricate carvings and adornments. Many called it the "Queen of Missions," as no other from the time came close to rivaling its splendor.

Life in San Antonio was difficult, to say the least. Apart from the natives outside the walls who didn't care too much for those who embraced the missionaries, there were other troubles to contend with. While the scant records of the mission do show more than 2,100 baptisms of natives, they also list burials of nearly twice that number due to several causes including disease and fighting. In 1783 alone, a smallpox epidemic killed more than two hundred natives who lived within the walls, with a second epidemic reducing their numbers even further.

Still, through hard work and determination, the mission flourished, leading many to state that even in Spain there were no churches its equal. The year 1794 saw the beginning of secularizing the missions of San Antonio, with full secularization becoming a reality in 1824. Although services continued to be held in the chapel, the rest of the mission began to slowly deteriorate.

In 1937 there was a renewed awareness of the history of Texas, specifically of the old missions. Grants and donations from organizations like the Daughters of the Republic of Texas allowed for the restoration of what was left of the mission. Four years later, the mission was honored when it became first a State Historic Site and then a National Historic Site.

The Ghosts...

There are a great many tales about Mission San José, some steeped in romanticism, others chilling in their nature. There may be more to the old mission than meets the eye, as the tales told have been passed from generation to generation, with a few new ones added by visitors.

One of the older tales of the mission has to do with what is called the "Window of Voices." Situated in the mission and unremarkable from other windows, the window holds a curious power to allow those who stand before it to hear the whispers and footsteps of the dead. According to the legend, standing in front of the window at the right time, visitors will hear a thousand whispered voices and the sounds of muffled footsteps. They are the voices of the Native Americans who died in or near the mission, their feet moving into the mission for a chance at divinity or salvation.

A second legend tells the tragic story of a young Spanish noble named Don Ángel de Léon who came to the mission, leaving his fiancé, Theresa, behind. Though they conversed by letters, their separation was torturous for them both. An Apache uprising ended young Ángel's life. When Theresa learned of her beloved's death, she lapsed into a deep depression. News came that the mission was nearing completion and all that remained was to have the great bells of the sanctuary cast. Theresa went to where the bells were to be made and threw her engagement ring into the molten metal, hoping that each ringing of the bells would let her love know that she'd been faithful to him. After that, she disappeared from the public eye, only coming to church to help the needy. Legend tells that she died smiling as the bells sounded their first ring. Legend also tells that the two lovers are reunited in the mission walls, and that they still walk together.

Apart from legends, both staff and visitors have had sightings of apparitions on the grounds. Most commonly seen is a man described as a monk who walks the convent courtyard on moonlit nights. Though he sometimes appears headless, he is always described as very tall, wearing the dark blue robes of a Franciscan monk, and walking through locked gates and walls.

Another apparition sighted — that seems to appear in two of the five missions — is that of a black dog. Appearing tiny at first, the creature reputedly grows to mammoth proportions, barking and foaming at anyone who comes near the mission with mischief on his mind. It has been sighted by more than a dozen people, all of whom describe it the same way, as having a broken chain around its neck and smelling of sulfur.

There is yet a third presence that has not only been seen during daylight hours, but has identified herself to park rangers and priests. An older woman, who introduced herself as Mrs. Huizar, approached a priest and asked when mass was to begin. The priest turned to ask another priest, but when he turned back the woman was gone. He asked if anyone knew a Mrs. Huizar, only to be told that she'd died some ten years earlier.

Present Day

A telephone call to the mission confirms that services are still held in the sanctuary, as they've been since 1840. The grounds are open to the public, however, and admission is free, though donations are greatly appreciated. Established as a National Historical Park in 1983, the mission is still owned by the Archdiocese of San Antonio and features a self-guided walking tour, historical markers, and a twenty-five minute video that is shown every half-hour about the history of the entire mission in the park. Visitors can also still see the stairway to the choir loft, each of the twenty-five risers hand-carved from a single live oak log and built without nails or pegs. The last reported paranormal event happened in the late 1990s, though almost everyone who enters the building reports feeling an overwhelming sense of peace.

Most apparitions were reported after dark — after the mission was closed for the day, but there have been others reported in broad daylight. Encounters with the headless priest and the large dog are usually reported in the convent courtyard, while Mrs. Huizar frequently visits the main sanctuary.

For more information on the Mission, call 210-932-1001 or visit its web site at http://www.nps.gov/saan/.

Nuestra Señora de la Purisma Concepción de Acuña

807 Mission Road
San Antonio, TX 78210

Mission Nuestra Señora de la Purísma Conceptción de Acuña.
Courtesy of Bradford and Jennifer Johnson.

There is a sense of safety inside her walls, the twin towers of her face imposing and protective at the same time. From within her towers, some can feel a priest's watchful eyes looking down upon them, while others feel the toil of those who worked the land around the mission. This was a place of belief, of dedication, and of reflection. More durable than the mortar holding the stones together, the human soul lingers on in places where it might feel safe.

Without much imagination, one can easily see why the Mission Nuestra Señora de la Purisma Concepción de Acuña casts such an imposing shadow. High towers with large windows, it has stood strong over two hundred years of hardship and abuse. Still, within its walls, there remains something that neither time nor bullets could wipe away: the dedication of those who bled for this land. While some might say the spiritual remains left behind are what makes a place holy, they also are what makes a place haunted.

The History

The original Mission Nuestra Señora de la Purisma Concepción was built in 1716 among the fearsome Tejas and Apache Indians of East Texas, near present day Nacogdoches. It was soon determined, however, that the location was unsuitable for missionary work due to constant attacks and an inhospitable environment. The mission was moved in 1730 to its present location between Mission San Antonio de Valero (The Alamo) and Mission San José.

Using the labor of converted natives and a unique construction process, it took nearly twenty-two years to complete. To honor Saint Mary, the virgin mother, the leaders of the mission explained that the mortar by which the stones were to be held together should be mixed with pure milk. The natives obeyed. The resulting mortar proved to be harder than the stones it was meant to hold together. Once completed, the church had near-perfect acoustics and twin towers on either side, giving it more the appearance of a heavily fortified fort than a church.

Along with the other missions of San Antonio, the Mission Concepción was secularized in February 1824. Although raids by hostile Apaches continued, Spanish settlers continued to arrive at the mission even after 1827.

On October 28, 1835, the first battle of the Texas revolution was fought near the mission. This so-named Battle of Concepción served as a warning to the Mexican armies that they really had no idea just who they were fighting and were ill-equipped to do so. The army of General Martín Perfecto de Cos attempted to take the soldiers of the Texan volunteer army with disastrous results. To begin with, the gunpowder they had was of such poor quality that most of the shots didn't even cross the distance to their targets. According to some reports, the Mexican bullets, rather than piercing the enemy, simply caused severe bruising and anger, and in some cases taunting and laughter. When it was all said and done, though superior in number, the Mexican army retreated leaving seventy-six wounded and dead. The Texans, led by James Bowie (for whom the giant double-edged knife was named), sustained only one casualty. Richard Andrews, known as Big Dick among the troops, ignored Bowie's orders to stay down behind the thick walls. When he stood up, he paid with his blood. A single shot to his side ensured a slow and agonizing death. The other Texans, however, followed orders. Trained in European warfare, the Mexican troops were unprepared by the Texans' guerilla tactics of hiding behind walls and shooting, and lost the battle.

The Texas troops stayed quartered at the mission for a while before moving on. In 1849, the mission became home to the United States Army, but then, in 1850, it was abandoned and desecrated. One visitor who passed by noted that the main church was being used to house cattle, and hordes of bats flocked through the ceilings. Filth covered the walls and floor. It seemed the church would be lost forever.

In 1859, however, the church title was given to the Brothers of Mary, who later founded San Antonio's St. Mary's University. It took them two years of hard work, but in 1861, the church was blessed and reopened. Twenty-six years later, after a great deal of toil and labor, the church was rededicated to Our Lady of Lourdes (the Immaculate Conception).

The Ghosts...

Whether they are called ghosts or angels, there seems to be something protecting all those who enter the mission. There are a great many stories about how those who stand within her walls feel safe, but even the hard-to-believe legends are, according to records, true. During one Indian raid, for example, the brothers threw the doors open to allow the converted natives inside. When the hostiles followed the very doorway, their horses stopped, as if held back by an unseen force. Those who made it inside fell to their knees, confident that it was the power of the Spanish God that saved them.

In addition, there have been a spate of apparitions sighted on the grounds; some resembling priests, others resembling Native Americans. The apparitions do not appear to interact with visitors, but have been seen going through the motions of their everyday life, as if watching a scene from a movie over and over again.

One restless spirit is also said to walk the grounds where he was killed so many years ago. Richard Andrews, who was cut down for his exuberance, has been sighted near the old battleground. Unlike the other apparitions, he does appear to acknowledge those who pass by, nodding in greeting before disappearing. Why he remains is a mystery.

Present Day

On November 10, 1978, the Mission Concepción, along with the other San Antonio Missions, became part of the San Antonio Missions National Park. For the next twenty years, the mission remained dormant until, in 1998, it reopened for services. The best preserved of the five missions (presumably because of the odd construction technique), the mission still operates as a parish. While sightings of apparitions are rare, visitors, parishioners, and even employees still occasionally report them.

For a true experience in Mission Concepción, a person should attend one of the weekly services that are held on Sundays at 10 a.m. However, if it's the paranormal you're seeking, apparitions of Native Americans and priests have been reported at all times throughout the year. Mostly sighted outside the church walls, there is occasionally a reported apparition of a monk in the bell tower or in the main sanctuary. Richard Andrews, however, most often appears on the anniversary of his death, October 28, on the actual battlegrounds.

For more information, call 210-534-1540 or visit its web site at http://www.nps.gov/saan/.

San Juan de Capistrano

9101 Graf Road
San Antonio, TX 78214

I t's late at night at the ruins of an old mission, its walls crumbled and decayed. Though the mission is closed for the evening, there is a man in a blue cloak who waits out front, his face grim. His purpose here is unknown. Perhaps he waits, protecting his beloved mission from vandals, or perhaps he simply stands sentry, waiting for someone who will never come. Whatever the case, he stands between the curious and the door, until he *vanishes* before their eyes, confirming the rumors that the old priest still walks the grounds.

For every failure, there is a victory, for every death, a birth. So might have been the motto of those who manned the Mission San Juan de Capistrano, for despite its many great achievements, its history is marred by failure and death. Portions of it were never completed, yet the pieces that were finished tell a miraculous story of engineering and agriculture. There is victory, even in defeat, at this old mission, and though those who built it are long since dead, their undying spirit seems to linger on.

The History

There are two distinct sides to the Mission San Juan de Capistrano's past; one is a tale of success, the other, one of woe. After being driven out of East Texas by the French, Spanish missionaries made their way to present-day San Antonio, encouraged by the successful Mission San Antonio de Valero. The missionaries encountered a tribe of Peyaye Indians, whom they found to be naturally friendly. The missionaries gave the natives gifts of rosary beads, tobacco, and pocketknives, earning their trust and friendship. They used the natives to help construct the

Mission San Juan Capistrano. *Courtesy of Bradford and Jennifer Johnson.*

first temporary buildings of a new mission. Named for Saint John Capistran, a Franciscan saint who'd been canonized in 1724, the Mission de San Juan de Capistrano was founded.

Almost from the beginning, the mission's life was one of hardship and death. Apache raids were continuous and, although they did not attack the mission itself, anyone caught outside its walls was likely to be killed in, what was reputed to be, the most brutal way. So bad were the raids that the Peyaye Indians, seeing no protection from the church, returned to their old ways and abandoned the mission.

After several attempts, and surrounded by armed guards, the clergy was able to reclaim roughly half of the deserted parishioners in 1738. The numbers of converted grew, but were quickly cut down again, this time by an epidemic of disease in 1739. It was during this time also that the archdiocese began getting reports, in the form of letters from the natives, of rampant abuse from the missionaries. It was later revealed that Governor Franquis de Lugo, had coerced the natives to write the letters, but the damage to the missionaries' reputations was already done.

By other accounts, however, the mission was quite successful. It was a self-sustaining native community with the church as the main focus of activities. Natives worked in shops, making everything from textiles to metal goods, and farmed the land outside the walls, always with a priest watching in case of attack from hostile forces. They were reputed to have had more than 3,500 sheep under their care and an entire ranch of cattle. The natives built a complex irrigation system that allowed them to grow sugar cane, pumpkins, and other produce, their surplus helping to support the other four missions in the area.

In 1756, a long, narrow church was completed and plans for another bigger church got underway almost immediately. Though construction began in 1760, the project was abandoned in 1780 with the building was only half completed. With Indian raids and disease rampant, the mission began limping along until being partially secularized in 1794. The government confiscated its cattle and the mission's resident father was reassigned. For a while, it became a sub-mission of the Mission San Francisco de la Espada. When it became completely secularized in 1824, the mission effectively died.

The year 1907 saw the rebirth of the Mission San Juan de Capistrano with Claretian Fathers taking over operations of it. After two years of repairing the ruined structures and rebuilding other fallen areas, the church was re-blessed and services were held once more.

The Ghosts...

For a mission with a past riddled with such tragedy and hardship, there are relatively few restless souls to be mentioned within her walls. While there have been sightings of Native Americans on the grounds, there is only one other apparition that has been reported. In the mid 1990s, a group was visiting the area and came to the mission after it had closed for the evening. Though it was getting dark, they still wanted to look around the building so they split up. The men went in one direction while their wives, certain that they shouldn't be there, stayed in front. The teenaged daughter of one of the couples stayed in the car. After a few minutes, the ladies in front of the mission claimed they felt uncomfortable, as if they were being watched. When they came back to the van, the daughter asked them about the man in the blue robe that had been standing behind them. No one saw the man, and he vanished before they found him. Others have seen the monk in blue as well.

Present Day

As with its sister missions, the Mission San Juan de Capistrano is still an active parish with services given in its tiny chapel. It's now a part of the Missions of San Antonio National Park and is open almost every day for visitors. In addition to the mission itself, there is also a self-guided nature trail at the mission for visitors.

While sightings of apparitions are few and far in between, they still do occur. Most common are the sightings of natives going about their daily life. The phantom monk has not been reported since the late 1990s, though he is reputed to walk the grounds at night.

As with the other parishes, the best time to visit is during the Sunday morning services so parishioners can get a true appreciation of the old church and spend a few hours looking around the site. Apparitions of Native Americans occur during both daytime and evening hours, but the mysterious blue-robed monk only seems to appear after dark near the front entrance, warning visitors that they should come back during normal operating hours. Why after-hours guests bothers him so is a mystery.

For more information, call 210-534-0749 or go to its web site at http://www.nps.gov/saan/.

San Francisco de la Espada

10040 Espada Road
San Antonio, TX 78214

P arents tell their children not to be afraid of the dark. There is nothing there in the dark that is not also there in the light. But sometimes, the darkness holds secrets, mysteries, and things that even adults fear. Though a place may be holy during the day, the nighttime gives pause to even the bravest of explorers. In some cases, it's because the dead walk. In others, there are beings placed to protect the buildings from anyone who ventures too near. During the day, all are welcome...*but stay away at night*.

In every neighborhood, there exists the one house or building that has a curious reputation. Whether deserved or not, buildings with ruined walls and dark windows naturally lend themselves to being the object of wonder and fear. Even if that building is a church, children fear it when the sun goes down. The warming rays of the sun reveal it for what it is, a building built of love and hardship, but at night, when shadows run long and the imagination takes over, even a church can be haunted.

The History

The history of the Mission San Francisco de la Espada is one fraught with tragedy. Beginning with an early mission in 1690 near present-day Weches, Texas, the missionaries had to fight an uphill battle. When the missionaries arrived, they unintentionally brought with them smallpox and the ensuing epidemic killed more than 3,300 people. The Nabedaches Indians, who were already mistrustful of outsiders, became hostile toward the missionaries. To make matters worse, the next two years were marked by a terrible draught, which the natives believed the Spanish brought down

Mission San Francisco de la Espada. *Courtesy of Bradford and Jennifer Johnson.*

upon them. After hostilities increased, with the promise of more aggressive action, the priests gathered what they could, burned the mission, and fled with their lives back to Monclova, Spain.

Never ones to give up easily, the monks returned in 1716 and rebuilt the mission atop the burned remains of the first one. Only three years later, they were again driven out, this time by the French. In 1721, the Spanish made one last futile effort to settle the area, but due to lack of interest by the Spanish government and the Archdiocese, and long memories of the natives, the mission was abandoned and the priests made their way to what is now San Antonio, hoping for an easier time of things.

In 1731, the missionaries arrived on the location of the present-day Mission San Francisco de la Espada to find Pacaos Indians. Cautious from their first encounters, they did their best to ensure friendship with the natives. The Pacaos, who were quite friendly, allowed them to stay and began working with them to build the mission. As in the past, there arose some conflict with the natives due to a smallpox epidemic in 1736, but by 1745 the first permanent structures of the missions were completed in the form of the aqueduct, the friary, and the sacristy. During construction, the natives learned to read and write as well as other skills, the most valuable of which turned out to be blacksmithing when things began to break and funding from the archdiocese was short.

In 1756, a small chapel was completed, restoring the hope of the mission's success, however more conflict was to come. Disease continued to be a problem, as were attacks from hostile natives. To add to the slowly souring morale, the church building collapsed in 1777. It wasn't long before the mission became secularized. In February 1824, faced with no other alternative, the priests surrendered the church to the government who seized most of the assets and parceled the land out to the natives and other settlers.

Natives continued to farm the land around the mission, which was used as a stronghold during the battle for Texas' independence from Spain. Just a few days before the Battle of Concepción in October of 1835, the Texas army, including commanders Travis and Bowie, used the mission as a rallying point. Still, the walls and structures continued to decay, victims of weather, neglect, and gunfire.

Between 1858 and 1907, a new priest, the Reverend Francis Bouchu, took up residence in the mission and set to work restoring the crumbling walls. For more than fifty years he labored, asking for assistance from the archdiocese. In 1907, they replied, agreeing that the mission should be rebuilt. The church was closed for repairs, and then re-blessed and reopened for mass and other services in 1915.

The Ghosts...

One of the more curious legends about the mission was that, when the missionaries arrived, the natives seemed to be expecting them. The chief of the tribe told the missionaries of a foreign woman who visited them a generation ahead of his. Through descriptions and drawings, the woman, who always dressed in blue, was determined to be Mary Coronel of Agreda, Spain, who wanted to be a missionary. According to legend, she never was able to leave her home, but prayed daily and had visions of foreign lands and natives. According to the natives, she appeared to them for many years until 1665, when she died in her home in Spain.

Much like other missions in San Antonio, there have been reports of apparitions of Native Americans. Visitors have reported one in particular, who appears in the main sanctuary, dressed in ceremonial clothes, often during the daylight hours.

One woman who works in the mission spoke of growing up near the old ruins. Her mother warned her of going near the mission at night because of the presence of a more frightening apparition—that of a large black dog. According to descriptions, the creature appears fierce, growling deeply, with a broken chain around his neck. It smells of sulfur, and chases trespassers off the property before disappearing. The similarities between it and the black dog that appears at Mission San José are striking.

Present Day

Visitors come to the Mission San Francisco de la Espada for many reasons. One is to see the living history in the form of the ruins that still stand. The wells, convent, and grainery are visible, as is the fortified tower and lime kilns. It's currently being restored by the Archdiocese of San Antonio, and is part of the Missions of San Antonio National Park. Weekly services are also still held on the premises.

As with the other missions in the park, the best time to visit one is for Sunday service, when one can truly appreciate the dedication and meaning of the mission. It's open daily from 9 a.m. to 5 p.m. for those who wish to see the ruins.

The apparitions continue unabated throughout the established visiting hours, with the ceremonially dressed native appearing at random times. However, it is not recommended that anyone attempt to glimpse the phantom dog, as the building is considered off-limits after-hours.

For information, call 210-627-2021 or visit its web site at http://www.nps.gov/saan/.

Haunted Museums

The old saying goes that history comes alive at museums. Whether it's a display on dinosaurs, the works of artists both past and modern, or an ancient mummy, there is a great deal to be learned about the past, present, and future. Thinking about all the pieces displayed, it's sometimes easy to forget that those items were once owned by people who lived, loved, and died around them. In some cases, those who wore the clothing or rode in the carriage displayed remain with them, even after death. Sometimes, it's not just the pieces, but also the building itself to which souls become attached. History, it seems, never dies, but lives on for those who seek it.

The Briscoe Western Art Museum

210 West Market Street
National Western Art Foundation
P.O. Box 90009
San Antonio, TX 78209

The Brisco Western Art Museum

Looking up from the street, the building itself is a work of art. The high arch of the doorway frames the steps in such a way as to be both inviting and awe-inspiring. Within lay the works of artists from across the west, pieces of equal ability to inspire with their beauty and fascinate the mind with their complexity. There is something else, however, that is unique to this building...*something* not listed in any brochure or pamphlet. It's not something brought in by the current inhabitants, nor is it something hanging on a wall or displayed in a case. It creeps though the stairwells, unseen by many but felt by most.

When a person dies a violent death, the spirit often cannot rest. If that murder goes unsolved, the victim has no resolution, no retribution. Such an act can leave a stain long after the house in which the tragedy occurred is gone...as if the blood soaked into the earth itself, permanently marking it as a place of grief and suffering. Although the original building has been gone for decades, such may be the case at the Briscoe Western Art Museum.

The History

San Antonio was young in 1837 and was a land of great opportunity. Immigrants from Germany, Mexico, and Ireland flocked to the city determined to make their fortune. One such newcomer was an Irishman named John McMullen. Already successful in Corpus Christi as a merchant with his partner James McGloin, McMullen arrived here alone—and determined. He built his home on what is now Market Street and began his new life.

McMullen prospered, becoming a prominent citizen of San Antonio, and keeping in contact with his close friend McGloin. In January 1853, however, his good life ended. He was found bound and gagged in his home, his throat cut. Burglary was determined to be the motive, and although people suspected his adopted son, a Mexican boy with blue eyes whose parents had died some years earlier, no arrests were made. To make matters worse, his son disappeared, leading some to conclude the child was another victim in the crime.

Just days later, as McMullen lay in state in his home, a distraught McGloin arrived on an exhausted horse. According to legend, he rode the beast nonstop until reaching his destination, whereupon the horse dropped dead. McGloin told a strange story, of how he was sitting in his home when the bloody apparition of his friend appeared before him. It seemed to be trying to tell him something, but he could not understand what. Without so much as another word, McGloin ran to his stable, saddled a horse, and left at a full gallop. He arrived too late to save McMullen, and could do nothing but mourn the loss of his dear friend.

In the early 1900s, the McMullen home was torn down and replaced in 1930 with a library. After some years, the library was moved, but the building was kept by the city to house a curious collection assembled by Mr. Harry Hertzberg. Now called the Hertzberg Circus Museum, the building contained numerous pieces from circuses from around the world. It continued to function until the late 1990s, when lack of funding forced the closing of the old building. The Hertzberg Circus Collection was acquired by the Witte Museum, where some pieces remain on display today, including the tiny coach that once belonged to Tom Thumb. The building, still owned by the public library, became a storehouse of unwanted items, records, and old books.

In May of 2007, a forty-year lease of the old Hertzberg Circus Museum building was given to the National Western Art Foundation. A multi-million dollar remodeling effort commenced for conversion into a new museum, this one focusing on western art. The Briscoe Western Art Museum is scheduled to open in the fall of 2009.

The Ghosts...

Over the years, there have been a great many sightings in the museum, though no one is really sure what they are. Some point to the pieces in the circus museum as having deceased performers attached to them, while others believe that Henry Hertzberg so enjoyed his collection that he continues to pop in from time to time to give it a looking-over. Most people, however, believe the restless soul in the building is John McMullen, still walking the grounds where his home once stood, stuck in limbo until his killer is identified. Those who spend time in the building say they've felt his presence and seen strange shadows darting between exhibits—*they knew they were never alone.*

Present Day

There are many remnants of the building's old purpose visible today. From the carved staircases to the impressive marble works and original fuse boxes, anyone privileged enough to walk through the halls can see that the building came from an era of different thinking. Built for both beauty and functionality, the building is deceptively large on the inside.

When the new owners took possession of the building, they knew its reputation for being haunted, but did not know by whom or what. As of this writing, construction was scheduled to begin for a fall 2009 opening. As construction always seems to stir up more than just dust, it will be interesting to see if McMullen—or anything else for that matter—still walks the building.

There is no "bad" time to visit a museum. However, although the phenomena occur periodically year-round, it seems to intensify during the month of January, when McMullen was murdered. The most talked-about place for sightings in the building is the massive former stacks room, where former employees have claimed to see shadows walk about as if the old bookshelves were still there.

For more information, call 210-832-3204 or visit their web site at http://www.briscoemuseum.org.

Witte Museum

3801 Broadway
San Antonio, TX 78209

The Witte Museum

Children flood the hallways, all entranced by the glimpses of older and foreign cultures. Mummies, Native Americans, and dinosaurs are topics of excited chatter as they dart back and forth between exhibits. It's a place of learning, culture, and history, one which children are happy to see. A glance to the right or left reveals a woman, a smile on her tired but determined face, watching the controlled chaos of school children as they talk excitedly amongst themselves. She no longer works here, but make no mistake—this is *her* museum.

When a person loves their job, they are happy in their place of work. When a person pours their life, their love, and their body and soul into their job, it stops being a place of work, and becomes a home. The reward of watching one's life work is often so great, the emotional attachment so strong, that it remains through joy and sorrow, after retirement, and even beyond death.

The History

What was to become the Witte Museum was actually the brainchild of one tenacious woman named Ellen Quillin. It was her notion that San Antonio needed a museum, and her efforts made that notion a reality. Through bake sales, asking for donations, and even selling bundles of bluebonnets, she was able to purchase what would be the museum's first collection, a group of displays by naturist H. P. Atwater. High school students made cases and two empty classrooms were used to display the pieces.

At the bequest of Alfred Witte, $75,000 was left after his death to the city, but he stipulated that the funds be used to build a museum named in honor of his parents. In 1926, the museum was completed and Ellen Quillin was named its first curator. Concerned that she might leave the post to start a family, the city was reluctant to place her in charge of the museum she started. She reassured them, however, promising not to marry during her first year in office, and assuring them that there would be no children. The museum, she explained, was her child.

Almost immediately after the building opened, Mrs. Quillin realized that it was far too small for her vision of what the museum should be. She began planning for expansions, first with the addition of wings on either side of the main building, and then with a second story.

During the Great Depression-era, the museum housed not only artifacts, but people as well. Those employees of the museum who could not afford housing, which was most of them, often lived in the building itself. A pair of Native Americans, who performed their traditional dances and ceremonies at the museum, even lived in the basement for a while. It was considered big news when, in the 1930s, the museum, realizing it could no longer sustain itself by selling flowers and cookies, decided to charge the then-outrageous admission fee of ten cents.

Ellen Quillin remained at her post for nearly forty years. Ellen was so dedicated to the museum that she continued showing up for work even ten years after being forced to retire in 1960. She was named Curator Emeritus, a title she held until her death.

Further expansion of the museum allowed for the moving or reconstruction of several historic homesteads on the site, as well as the first city-funded public school building, which is still used as a classroom. While breaking ground for these new attractions, workers discovered artifacts from a Native American campground. For a time, famed San Antonio potter and artist Harding Black taught classes from the site, as well as producing his own pottery for sale. During one late evening, Black looked up to see a small fire start in the construction area of the new second floor. He rushed up the stairs and was able to put out the blaze, saving the museum, but he claimed the spirits of the Native Americans on the site led him to look up at just that time.

The Ghosts...

Ask nearly anyone in the museum and the answer will be the same. Yes, Mrs. Quillin is still around. She has been sighted repeatedly by museum patrons and employees, and adults and children alike. So much paranormal activity, along with the sightings, have occurred that in 1999, the San Antonio-based Institute of Paranormal Investigations conducted an after-hours hunt on the premises. The results of that investigation were inconclusive, but did include a few EVPs (disembodied voices) and a few odd photos. The investigators also had several personal experiences while there.

Of the phenomena reported, by far the most interesting is the apparent full-body apparition of Mrs. Quillin herself. However, the staff has reported hearing footsteps in empty rooms, the sounds of file cabinets being opened and closed, and dark shadows that dart about.

Far from being the only resident spirit, Mrs. Quillin is joined by an unknown number of entities. In certain places of the museum, people have reported feeling a "presence" while in others employees have had objects move and heard voices. One phenomenon involved telephone calls to the security station from inside the building. The trouble was the security guard was the only one on duty at the time, and the rest of the building was empty. That particular security guard quit his job over the issue. Guards have also heard the sounds of someone trying the doors around the Butterfly Garden area, though, through the glass, they can plainly see no one is there.

Present Day

The Witte now is a thriving environment for learning. Included in their exhibits are textiles, pieces of Texas history, exhibits from Native American history (including a buckskin dress cut from a body at Wounded Knee), a mummy, and dinosaurs. The tree-house exhibit is a hands-on learning experience for children, and there are plans to expand even further in the near future. There is even an exhibit of live animals in the museum.

Mrs. Quillin still makes frequent appearances, as do whoever else might be walking the museum hallways. People can meet Mrs. Quillin's "ghost," if they so choose, by attending the "A Gallery of Ghosts" performance, in which an actress portraying the museum's founder relates stories of her life–*and afterlife*–in the museum.

Although many of the places where phenomena occur are off-limits to the public, one should not despair. There are very active sites all through the museum. Mrs. Quillin is most often sighted going up and down the left stairwell, but has also often been seen walking past the entryway door. Another presence has been felt, and, according to a psychic, loves the space by the Texas by Candlelight Bedroom. Just down the hall is a room exhibiting furniture made by hand. Behind one of the temporary flats, however, is a large stained glass window, called the Lord Byron window, which was donated to the museum by a family after the death of their son. Although it's not visible to most who walk into the room, it's believed that this window has some entity attached to it.

The most active areas in the museum, however, are open to employees only. In their History Storage room, heavy footsteps have been heard moving up a hollow ramp. Next door, in the Textile Storage room, shadows dart about on two aisles, and paranormal investigators have reported seeing bright flashes of light under the door when the room was closed and the electricity turned off. Up the stairs, in the Pottery Storage room, there is often an apparition of Mrs. Quillin, which stands to reason as it was her old office. Even the Photo Storage room and vault have been sites for some very strange occurrences. Odd as it may seem, however, two sites that have apparently no activity are the displays of the dress cut from a Native American woman during the Battle of Wounded Knee and the Anthropology Storage room, although their life-sized bear totem can be quite startling when the lights are just turned on.

As for when to experience or see something supernatural, so many occurrences have been reported at the Witte that it has been theorized that phenomena happens all the time, but the museum is often too busy for it to be noticed. Apart from getting a job at the museum and working late at night, it seems the best time to visit are on days of the "Gallery of Ghosts" performances—keep your eyes and ears open for anything out of the ordinary.

For more information, call 210-357-1900 or visit its web site at http://www.wittemuseum.org.

The Institute of Texan Cultures

801 South Bowie Street
San Antonio, TX 78205-3296

The Institute for Texan Cultures

M any cultures came together to create the state of Texas. San Antonio is a mirror of that cultural diversity, with nearly every nationality represented in one form or another. Within the walls of the Institute of Texan Cultures, pieces of the state's rich history stand as proud reminders of where the people came from and of what the city is made. And, as is the case with many such places, there are pieces of people left behind... *shadows of the past that linger and let people know that the past is never truly gone.*

Many museums have their resident ghosts, whether attached to the pieces in their collection or to the land on which it was built. In many cases, one's passion for the museum lives on long after those who built it have passed away. The spirits could be something as fleeting as a glimpse, as random as a scent, or as overt as an apparition, but they're there and they add to the oral tradition of the people the museum represents. The stories told by any people do more than relate a history; it also reveals much about their culture. At the Institute of Texan Cultures, the people represented cover every ethnicity and creed, coming together to form one people: Texans.

The History

The Institute of Texan Cultures was born of political scandal and became a landmark in the city. When the 1968 Hemisfair was announced, then-President and Texan Lyndon Baines Johnson declared San Antonio to be the perfect spot for the festivities. Along with Governor John Connelly, Johnson scoured the city until he found what he determined to be the perfect location for the plaza. There was only one problem, however—the site was already occupied with low-rent housing and ethnic neighborhoods.

Declaring eminent domain, the government set to work displacing entire families from the neighborhood. The original communities of Chinese, Africans, and Irish were razed in an effort to prepare for the massive festival, bankrupting many. Only one known success story came out of the displacement in the form of a man who sold fried chicken in the neighborhood. Because his business was bulldozed, he was forced to rent another location. His chicken proved to be so popular that it became the national Churches Fried Chicken chain. Most, however, were not so lucky. Many historic buildings were demolished or moved. Had it not been for staunch political support, what is now known as La Villita might have fallen before the bulldozers as well.

In 1967, construction began on what was to be called the Texas Pavilion. The massive structure was intended, ironically, to show off the diverse cultures of the city—the same cultures the government had wiped out to build it. It was completed in 1968, in time for the Hemisfair, and then was turned into a permanent museum.

By 1971, the Institute of Texan Cultures was in full bloom under the direction of R. Henderson Shuffler, who maintained an apartment in the building and often worked late nights and through weekends. It continued to grow through the generous donations of artifacts and support from University of Texas San Antonio.

The Ghosts...

The Institute of Texan Cultures has, in addition to some truly fascinating exhibits, quite a few stories attached to it—many of which reference former employees. While there does not seem to be any malevolent spirits within the walls, there are a few things that can be a bit disquieting. There are three "main" ghost stories of the institute.

The first, and most famous, story revolves around an impressive artifact in the form of a horse-drawn hearse from Castroville, Texas. Built in 1898 by the Saville Company in Cincinnati, Ohio, the hearse was brought to Texas where it was used by the town until 1930. The hearse was used not only for bringing hundreds of dead bodies to their final resting place, but also for the purpose of bootlegging bourbon. A hidden compartment that lay beneath the casket rollers made a perfect place to hide bottles, as no one would dare stop a hearse. When it arrived at the institute, it soon became clear that there was *something* attached to it. A security guard passed by the hearse one evening to discover its doors open. He closed the doors, making sure to lock the complicated latch system. When he returned, the doors were open again.

Paranormal investigators have examined the hearse and have recorded a strange animalistic growl from below the struts, as well as photographed apparitions around it.

The second, and most constant, haunting is believed to be that of the institute's original director, R. Henderson Shuffler. Many who work in the building have smelled the distinctive cherry-scented pipe smoke for which Shuffler was known, even though smoking has been banned in the building for twenty years. Always by the library, Shuffler is believed to sit, as was his custom, in the after-hours on weekends.

The third story is that of a man named Gerald Fritz who once worked on the ground crew of the institute. Gerald, who was slightly mentally handicapped, was well liked by the staff and always greeted them whenever he saw them. He was known for his affectation of counting his change and for being such a kind soul. One Monday morning, as she approached the building, an employee noticed Gerald standing by the back entrance. It struck her as odd since, instead of wearing his usual uniform of cover-alls, he was smartly dressed in a suit with a beautiful blue tie. After greeting him, she went inside and to the break room. When she inquired what the occasion was that he was dressed up, she was met with dumbfounded looks and informed that there was no way she could have seen hime. He'd *died* the previous Friday. That same day, Gerald was seen by another employee counting his change by the vending machines, dressed in a suit with a blue tie. When he described Gerald's clothing, he was informed that those were the clothes in which he'd been buried.

Over the years there have been other apparitions, one where a guard saw only the lower half of a woman dressed in red and another in which a janitor reported that all the bathrooms on the top floor of the building flushed at the same time and were running with blood. The latter quit her job and refused to reenter the museum, although no evidence was ever found of such an event.

Recently, however, there has been another apparition that some suspect may be tied to some of the pottery in the "Creation Cosmos" exhibit, a cave-like structure that showcases pottery from the Cato Indians and compares it to that of natives from South America. Twice, and by two separate individuals, a woman in a buckskin dress has been sighted either in or near the opening of the cave. Though her identity is uncertain, she is clearly Native American.

Present Day

The museum has continued to grow over the years into one of the most impressive collections of diverse cultures in the world. Once a month, it hosts the Naturalization Ceremonies, in which resident aliens become citizens of the United States. It features items of interest for every age, including specialty exhibits on such folklore fascinations as dragons and Bigfoot. When the Creation Cosmos exhibit opened, a Cato shaman came to perform a sweetgrass blessing on the space in hopes of laying any souls attached to the pottery displayed to rest. While Gerald has not been seen since his 1992 visit, leading many to believe it was simply his way of saying goodbye, the hearse has been featured on television programs about the paranormal and has become a sort of initiation for new security guards. The inside of the hearse also still has a peculiar odor—that of the dead with sachets of sweet smelling flowers to try to mask the smell. Weekend evenings are still greeted by the scent of cherry pipe tobacco.

Most of the paranormal activity takes place in areas away from the public eye. The hearse only seems to misbehave after closing time, and Shuffler seems to stick to his ritual of smoking his pipe after-hours in the library. As for the native woman in the cave, her appearances are a recent development, but she has been most often sighted at the entrance of the cave and in the quiet "reflection chamber." Paranormal activity aside, the best days to visit vary, but include Naturalization Days; the ceremony is quite moving. The museum is open to the public on Tuesdays through Saturdays from 10 a.m. to 6 p.m. and noon to 5 p.m. on Sundays. It also hosts special events at holidays, including a Halloween event featuring the institute's ghost stories as told by resident folklorist Rhett Rushing.

To reach the museum, call 210-458-2330 or visit its web site at http://www.texancultures.utsa.edu.

The Spanish Governor's Palace

105 Plaza de Armas
San Antonio, TX 78205

The Spanish Governor's Palace. *Courtesy of Bradford and Jennifer Johnson.*

No matter the age, it is a palatial estate. Hidden from the outside world by a plain white stucco wall are antiques, trappings of power and wealth, and a garden the likes of which may have been common during the early years of Texas, but today have become a curiosity. As one walks through the rooms, there is a sense of pride and history, but there is something else as well. In San Antonio, even places of luxury seem to have been built around tragedy, giving birth to not only legends, but whispers of ghosts as well.

There are many places that, from the outside, visitors may not know exactly what they are looking at. For all intents and purposes, the building that stands across from City Hall is just a large white block, a stucco and masonry structure that looks like many in San Antonio with a plaque on the wall and bars over a window. Inside, however, one realizes why *National Geographic* magazine called it one of the most beautiful houses in Texas. While such a claim may seem to be a matter of opinion, one thing is irrefutable: This house and the land on which it stands have borne witness to all manner of deaths and tragedy. As with many other places in San Antonio, here the dead refuse to rest.

The History

What is now known as the "Spanish Governor's Palace" is believed to have been constructed well before the date on its keystone, which is 1749. Its palatial appearance aside, the building was, in fact, never occupied by a governor, Spanish or otherwise. It was built as a home to the captain of the Spanish Presidio in charge of safeguarding the Mission San Antonio de Valero, which later became known as The Alamo. Exactly why it came to have its curious misnomer is something of a mystery, but it's a name that most in San Antonio have come to embrace.

During its time as home of the Presidio Captain, the building saw more than its share of bloodshed in the form of executions, battles, and, according to some, at least one murder. When San Antonio became the capital of Spanish Texas, the building became the seat of that branch of government. For more than one hundred years, it served its purpose and sat respected by the people of the city.

However, as with most buildings, once it outlived its usefulness in one form it was recycled into another. At one point in its long life it was a bar. Another period saw it used as a school. Still another saw it as a humble merchant front, housing such businesses as a cleaner and a tailor. It wasn't until 1928 that the city of San Antonio purchased the building, and it began its return to its rightful place in history. In 1962, it was reopened as a museum and registered as a Texas historic landmark.

The Ghosts...

There are two main stories of specters that haunt the hallways of the old Presidio Captain's home; one surrounding the beautiful fountain on the patio, the other concerning the curious tree outside. While there is no way to prove one, the other is hard to dispute.

The first legend varies, depending upon who tells it. In one instance, the body of a murdered girl was hidden in the fountain. In the second, a young girl was drowned in its waters. However it happened, there have been numerous reports of sightings of a young Spanish girl sitting near the fountain weeping. There have also been reports of objects moving within the ten rooms of the building and sounds of a woman's soft cries being heard during the night.

The tree outside, however, is not the subject of conjecture, but is instead the stuff of legend. The tree was, as the story goes, the site of so many hangings that the branches dipped and now grows low. More curious, however, are the patterns in the tree's bark. Even those who do not know the tree's macabre history often remark that the swirls and knots look disturbingly like faces howling in pain. According to legend, the faces began appearing after the first man was hanged, with new faces appearing for each subsequent victim.

Present Day

From 1929 to 1930, local architects and the San Antonio Conservation Society rescued the building from its crumbling state. The ten rooms were furnished with period furniture, giving visitors a glimpse into the past lives of those who lived there. It stands as the last remaining example of Spanish aristocracy from that time period in Texas, making it all the more special. It's currently operated by the San Antonio Parks & Recreation Department as a museum with a performance group that presents scenes from the time period once a month.

According to the staff, the hauntings continue, though some seem to tell the stories from rote memorization. When asked, they will tell the stories of the weeping girl and the tree with the faces of the damned, but finding a person who has had a recent experience has proven difficult.

The tree is visible any day of the week, though the weeping girl is reputed to appear near closing time. The best times it seems to visit the museum is during its open hours of 9 a.m. to 5 p.m. Monday through Saturday. On Sunday it opens an hour later. To experience the "living history" group, La Compañia de Cavallarìa del Real Presidio de San Antonio de Bexar, one should make plans to visit on the final Sunday of each month.

For more information, call 210-224-0601 or visit its web site at http://www.sanantonio.gov/sapar/spanishgovernorspalace.asp.

5

Other Haunted Hotspots

L ike any other large city, San Antonio has a great number of places in which spirits seem to like to hang about. Theaters, parks, gardens, and other places that most might not think would be haunted have their share of stories for anyone who'd like to hear them. Ghosts of children, soldiers, actors, and even animals dot the city map with stories that combine to give San Antonio another important piece of its culture. For those wishing to experience the true San Antonio life, these places are essential as they make up a crucial part of what makes San Antonio what it is. And, like many other places, when people walk within these places, they are never truly alone.

San Antonio College

**1300 San Pedro Avenue
San Antonio, TX 78212**

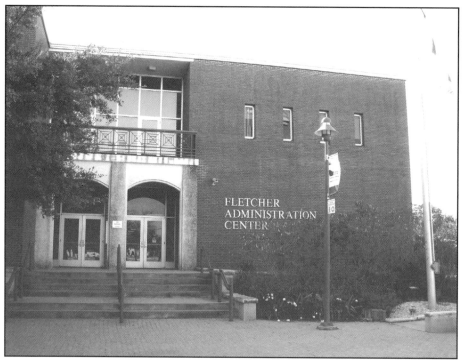

San Antonio College Administration Building. *Courtesy of Bradford and Jennifer Johnson.*

San Antonio College was founded in 1925, still a relative youngster compared to many of the other colleges in the area. What it lacks in age, however, it makes up for in educational advantages. The original name of University Junior College was changed in 1948 to San Antonio College, and the institute continued to grow. From a student body of more than five hundred students to the present-day yearly enrollment of more than 30,000 students, the college has continued its tradition of serving the community well.

Along the way, however, it seemed to pick up a few otherworldly residents. Stories have surfaced from time to time about phantom noises, apparitions, and strange happenings within the college's many buildings. Faculty, staff, and students seem know that there are certain places where even the brave do not tread alone, where the shadows run just a bit longer, and where the dead walk. Whether caused by tragedy or by a love of the institute, these stories come together to paint a portrait of a living college, one that thrives in its academics—and one that has more than its share of "school spirit."

Koehler Cultural Center

The History

Otto Koehler was a German immigrant who came to the United States in 1872. Living in St. Louis, he honed his skill at making beer in the Griesedieck breweries. By the time he arrived in San Antonio in 1884 he was a master brewer. Koehler was, in fact, one of the driving forces behind organizing the San Antonio Brewing Association. When Otto Koehler selected the site for his new home, rumor has it that it was because the hilltop lot allowed him to see the Lone Star Brewing Company, which he managed, with no obstructions. Whether true or not, what remains is the massive structure he built. In 1901, Koehler lived in what is now called Laurel Heights.

Built by Carol Von Seutter, the home was immense. Victorian styled and fitting Koehler's status, it featured large columns, sweeping arches, and an enormous basement that held a single-lane bowling alley.

Koehler resigned his position in the Lone Star Brewery and took over operations of what is now the Pearl Brewery. In 1914, Koehler suffered a violent death at the hands of

Koehler Cultural Center. *Courtesy of Bradford and Jennifer Johnson.*

someone alleged to be his lover, who shot him on the south side of the house. His wife Emma took over operations at the brewery until her death.

Otto Koehler had a twin brother, whose son was also named Otto. The young Koehler spent much of his youth with his aunt and uncle. When she passed away in 1943, he and his wife Marcia moved into the mansion, and Otto followed in his uncle's footsteps, taking over the Pearl brewery. But the tough times were not over, as the second Otto was rumored to have killed his mistress inside the house as well, though most sources claim the story is not true. He continued working for the Pearl brewery until his death in 1969.

In 1971, the Koehler mansion was given to the San Antonio Union Junior College District for use as a cultural center. For a time it housed the business offices of the San Antonio Art League until they outgrew their space.

The Ghosts...

There are reportedly several ghosts that roam the grounds of the Koehler estate, two of whom are named Otto Koehler. The elder Koehler returns to the scene of his death and wanders the hallways of his beloved home. His appearances are often marked with heavy boot steps and doors that open and close by themselves. The younger Koehler, on the other hand, has been only heard, but not seen, in the building. His voice travels in whispers, according to reports, calling out names or talking just softly enough that it's difficult to make out what he is saying.

The third restless spirit in the Koehler House has been identified as Emma Koehler. She has been sighted on many occasions in many different areas of the house. She is believed to be a benevolent spirit, who only wishes to stay in her home.

Other phenomenon encountered includes the feeling of being watched and presences that accompany people throughout the house. While such phenomena can be unsettling, those who have experienced them don't believe the spirits to be in any way harmful.

Present Day

Today, the beautiful old mansion is a part of San Antonio College and serves several purposes. The upper floors are currently used as office space whereas the bottom floor can be rented out for weddings, conferences, meetings, or any other type of celebration. Its ornate carvings, tile work, and elegant style hearken back to a bygone era, making the home a source of awe and respect for students. Presences are still felt in the house on a fairly consistent basis, and while some may doubt the veracity of its haunted reputation, those who have experienced the phenomena firsthand have no doubt.

The Koehler Cultural Center is not considered a "public" building; visitors do not generally just walk in and mill about. While the facilities can be rented for various purposes, it's still considered an office building, albeit a beautiful one. Students are taken past the building when touring the campus, and those who wish to tour the building can do so by setting up a tour with the main campus administration. The unexplained sounds of footsteps and whispering come from largely downstairs while Emma Koehler has been sighted all over the building. Always appearing after-hours, she has been seen most frequently on the stairwell and in the parlor.

To schedule a tour, call 210-731-6761. More information is available on its web site at http://www.accd.edu/sac/koehler/default.htm.

McAllister Auditorium

The History

In 1946, the generosity of Walter Williams McAllister, Sr. allowed San Antonio College to exist, as it was he who purchased the first tract of land for the campus. When construction was complete and classes commenced, the massive theater building was christened in his name. His tradition of helping educational institutes continued through his son, Walter McAllister, Jr., who also purchased land so the college could expand.

The theater itself was massive in structure, able to seat over 1,000 audience members on its two levels. In addition to the proscenium stage and upper balcony, the structure also included an interesting addition to its architecture. A full-sized pipe organ was built right into the wall, allowing its sounds to reverberate throughout the building.

Since opening in 1956, the theater has hosted lectures and theatrical productions alike, as well as musical performances by the college. Renovation took place, updating the lighting system, the seating, and other important elements for the comfort of patrons and to be able to have more impressive productions.

The Ghosts...

Whatever else may take place in the theater, whether dramatic interpretations, lectures, or musical performances, most who work there know that actors aren't the only things hiding behind the curtains. While some don't like to talk about the strange goings-on, others who have had their own experiences are more than happy to discuss the theater's resident spirits. While many of the phenomena can be summed up by prickly feelings of creeping flesh and cold spots, there are some who have seen apparitions.

Of the two manifestations, the one most often sighted is that of a woman. Described as an elderly lady, she is most often seen in the prop and costume storage areas and by the shop. She wears a long white gown, and has been reported to interact with those who encounter her, even holding a conversation with a student who didn't realize he was talking to a non-corporeal being. When he asked who the old lady upstairs was, he was greeted with a retelling of the encounters with her.

The second apparition is none too friendly, according to those who have seen him. Identified as a former theater manager from the 1970s, he is an imposing figure at well over six feet tall and hefty. He is balding with wild curly hair on the sides. He once appeared in the lighting booth during a late rehearsal, when tensions were high and the crew was getting frustrated. The witness saw him, laughing maniacally as if to admit his role in causing the trouble before disappearing. Rehearsal was shortened that night.

McAllister Auditorium. *Courtesy of Bradford and Jennifer Johnson.*

Present Day

As a part of the San Antonio College campus, McAllister Auditorium is a busy theater, as its used by the theater, music, and communications departments. In addition to full-length productions, each fall the theater participates in a theater awareness program for elementary school children to build their interest in the arts.

The theater's permanent patrons, however, never leave. Still wandering the backstage area, the old woman continues to be seen, and while the former manager has not been seen in a while, his presence is still felt. The prickly feelings continue, as anyone who works in the building can attest.

To enjoy the fine productions performed in the theater, one need only to buy a ticket. The schedule of productions is listed on the theater's website, and discounts are given for students and children. Most paranormal activity, however, is limited to places where paying patrons do not go. The old woman seems to stay in the backstage area, preferring to be out of the limelight, while the former manager most often shows up to laugh at the other production crew. The best way to experience the theater from a haunted point of view is to audition for one of their many productions. As auditions are only open to students, it seems that the only way to experience this school spirit is to have... school spirit.

To purchase a ticket or for more information, call 210-733-2715 or visit its web site at http://www.accd.edu/sac/theatre/theatrespeech/McAllister/McAllister.html.

San Antonio Botanical Gardens

**555 Funston Place
San Antonio, TX 78209**

San Antonio Botanical Gardens Carriage House

mongst the trails and plant life, people come to find peace. Some come to watch birds or to experience as much of nature as possible. Others come to learn about the native foliage of Texas, or to see plants they would never otherwise see. But squirrels and birds are not the only things that move in the bushes. Down the trails where trees drape the skyline like fingers, it's possible to encounter more than flowers and birds...*you could also encounter the dead.*

In many cases, hauntings are not the product of violent deaths or tragedy, but of love and happiness. Just as a tragedy can leave a scar, a life of love for a location can leave a similar mark, replaying the happy times or even allowing a visit from the past. It's very rare, however, to find a place where the tragic and the wonderful coincide. Whether a building was built on the spot or brought from another location, the stones hold memories, and no matter what sits on a site now, the land never forgets. In either case, the land has the distinction of being haunted.

The History

Though it may seem difficult to believe, the lush gardens and greenery that are now the San Antonio Botanical Garden was, at one time, a large limestone quarry. Essentially a giant hole in the ground, the quarry operated for many years until 1877. It was then that the quarry was turned into a water-works system by the contracting firm of J. B. LaCoste and Associates. Six years later, it was sold to G. W. Brackenridge.

By 1899, the water-works was largely abandoned. With the citizens relying on wells instead of the water-works, Brackenridge gave the land to the city of San Antonio, where it sat unused for more than seventy years.

In the late 1960s, a plan was brought before the city council by Mrs. R. R. Witt and Mrs. Joseph Murphy to create a public garden center. The following year, with the plan put before the public, San Antonio citizens voted to allocate more than a quarter of a million dollars to the construction of the center. Other grants soon followed, raising enough money for the groundbreaking ceremony in 1976. Four years later, the garden opened to the public.

As the years passed, additions were made to the gardens such as a conservatory, children's attractions, and a sensory garden for the blind. It continued to grow, attracting visitors from around the globe as a place where people could experience the plant world and educate themselves in the importance of plant life.

During the late 1980s, an historic building was brought to the site and, with it, what seemed to be a spectral visitor. Originally built in 1896, the Sullivan Carriage House was used as stables by the Sullivan family until the 1960s, at which time it was willed to the San Antonio Archdiocese. A series of events and changes of ownership found the carriage house belonging to the Botanical Gardens, who disassembled and moved it, brick by brick, and then reassembled the historic building for use as the entrance to the gardens, a gift shop, and a tiny restaurant. After many years, it finally opened to the public in 1995.

The Ghosts...

The staff know the stories, and although they are told in an unofficial capacity, they are told nonetheless. Formal gardens and displays are not the only things to be experienced. There are, it seems, two restless spirits that inhabit the park, and though neither is malicious, both can be somewhat startling to the uninitiated.

The first apparition seen by staff and visitors alike is that of a little girl darting about the Sullivan Carriage House. Although appearing as a child, the ghost is believed to be that of Miss Sullivan, who died at the age of ninety. Identified from photos of Miss Sullivan's youth, it's commonly believed that the carriage house was a place of great happiness during her childhood and that what remains is an impression from that joyous time. It appears then, when each limestone block was painstakingly reassembled, the craftsmen brought something other than the building with them.

The second apparition has startled more than a few guests and employees. Believed to be a Calvary soldier, this apparition gallops on his horse throughout the gardens and disappears through a wall shared with Fort Sam Houston. His appearance is made all the more startling due to the fact that he always appears headless. Just who he was in life is unknown, but it's a safe bet that his death was violent and occurred during one of the many battles that took place in San Antonio's bloody past.

Present Day

Although the city of San Antonio still owns the Botanical Garden, it's operated by a non-profit organization and supported through donations and sales from the gift shop. Now a sprawling 33-acre property, it features a Japanese garden, rose gardens, water conservation areas, and even a Texas Native Trail. It's available for student groups and private parties, and is open every day of the year with the exception of Christmas and New Years Day. There are group tours available and it's accessible for every age group and mobility.

Sightings of both the little girl and the headless rider happen often enough that staff know immediately what a person is talking about when they ask about the ghosts, though the latter hasn't occurred in several years.

The best time to visit the botanical garden is in the full bloom of springtime, though there really is no "bad" time to visit. No matter the time of year, there are places of beauty throughout the facility. The spectral visitors appear at random, in both daylight and darkness. Those who hope to glimpse the young Miss Sullivan have the best chance inside the main carriage house and around the backside. She's also been seen looking out the upstairs windows. The headless rider, on the other hand, is most often sighted at the far back corner of the "Texas Native Trail."

For more information, call 210-207-3250 or visit its web site at http://www.sabot.org.

Aggie Park

6205 West Avenue
San Antonio, TX 78231

Aggie Park. *Courtesy of Bradford and Jennifer Johnson.*

sk any Texan and they'll say that Texas is football country. College football especially brings an unparalleled furor that few can comprehend. In a place where people come, united by the love of a school and their beloved football team, something lingers. It walks the halls, making its presence known to anyone who walks within the building, letting them know that being an Aggie doesn't stop when you die. Aggie pride goes on forever.

Texas A&M has a longstanding tradition of pride and education. Throughout the south, one would be hard pressed to find a person not familiar with "Aggie Jokes" or with the famous maroon and white banners. From sports to academics, Texas A&M has a great deal of which to be proud and Texas A&M students are more loyal than any in the world to their alma mater. Whether graduating from the famed Aggie Corps or simply students, alumni of the great institution have a sense of pride unequaled by any other. Small wonder, then, that land dedicated as a meeting place for alumni and students should lend a different meaning to the phrase "school spirit."

The History

In the late 1930s, a dairy farmer named Henry Weir was approached by a group of Texas A&M alumni about renting out roughly three acres of his land for their annual picnic. Weir agreed, setting a precedent for years to come. His end of the bargain was to mow the grass on the three acres, on which the Aggies would meet, talk football, barbecue, and drink beer.

The year 1943 brought a change in the arrangement. Weir, it seemed, was retiring from the dairy business. When the Aggies heard that their beloved spot was in jeopardy, ten of the members pooled their money and purchased the 3.3-acre parcel for the then-staggering price of $999. They called the place Aggie Memorial Park, in honor of past alumni who could no longer partake in the revelries. In true Aggie fashion, the first permanent structure to go up on the site was an enormous brick barbeque pit. It wasn't until 1953, however, that an actual meeting hall was erected, using parts, money, and labor from donations and volunteers.

One year later, the San Antonio A&M Club re-dedicated Aggie Park to fallen Aggie soldiers. It became more than just a park, but a symbol of Aggie Pride that was felt throughout the state. In 1979, the San Antonio A&M Club moved all of its operations to the facility, including weekly luncheons and meetings of the Aggie Wives Club.

The Ghosts...

Whenever one talks about the alumni of Texas A&M, one characteristic that is always mentioned is the indomitable Aggie Spirit. At Aggie Park, that phrase may just have literal significance. Believed to be haunted by former members of the A&M Club, the building has become host to a large number of phenomena.

In an interview with Docia Williams for her 1997 book *When Darkness Falls*, several members related a number of quite interesting events ranging from cold spots to apparitions. Follow-up interviews revealed that lights have been reported to go on and off at random while objects have been removed from their locations, only to resurface later in strange places. There have been sightings of the figure of a man and strange shadows reported by men, women, employees, and visitors alike.

Some say that the activity is the result of a funeral that was held in the building while others point out that the phenomena predates any wakes or funeral services. However, the ground on which the building sits was discovered to have been once used as a Native American campground with several burial sites included. Some believe the presences are a direct result of building on that land. Most, however, refer to the haunting in a different way. Strange things or not, it's just another manifestation of the Aggie Spirit.

Present Day

Aggie Park today is a facility funded by the generosity of alumni and patrons. It features a large multipurpose room and often hosts banquets, weddings, and other types of get-togethers. The Aggie Wives hold their weekly luncheon on Mondays, with other functions planned throughout the week.

Still, as recent as April 2007, the activity continues. According to one secretary, many of the Aggie Wives are afraid of what may lurk in the building and won't go into the facility alone. Others, however, have gotten used to the strange goings on.

There's really no telling what's going to happen when a group of A&M alumni get together. However, the best time of year to go and honor the dead is on April 21, when the Aggies do just that. A general muster is called with a ceremony that is something humbling to behold. It's during this ceremony that the Aggies who died the previous year are given their honors. It may be that the bugler's mournful rendition of Taps calls them to this place, giving them a place to meet for camaraderie for all eternity.

For information or to reserve the facility, call 210-341-1393 or visit its web site at http://www.aggiepark.com.

San Pedro Playhouse

800 West Ashby Street
P.O. Box 12356
San Antonio, TX 78212

San Pedro Playhouse. *Courtesy of Bradford and Jennifer Johnson.*

An actor stands up on a stage, the spotlight focused for the delivery of his monologue, the one that brings an audience to tears. It is only a rehearsal, he knows, but he has to get it right. Through the halo of light, in the back of the auditorium, he sees an older couple sitting in the audience. A blink of the eye and they are gone. Was it a trick of the light, he wonders, or has he finally seen what so many others before him have seen? He may have been a skeptic, but here, in this place, magic can and does happen. Who is he to say that the spirit of the theater is not a metaphorical thing, but real entities that love the stage just as much as he? He clears his throat and delivers his lines, confident that the sighting has been a sort of blessing.

The theater has long held its own traditions; the smell of the greasepaint, the roar of the crowd...and *the ghosts*. Every theater seems to have its own set of ghost stories. To not have a ghost in a theater is considered bad luck. Ghosts appear in places of passion, high energy, love, and pain. For a theater to be devoid of such emotions is unfathomable. It stands to reason, then, that any theater worth its curtain would have a few spirits hanging around. Whether they be former actors returning to answer their cues, patrons who just can't get enough of the show, or even some other patron spirit that arrived attached to a prop, they find their homes in the dark corners of the theaters, and the actors treat them with respect and reverence. In turn, the spirits allow productions to proceed without incident. After all, the show must go on.

The History

While the building itself only dates back to 1925, the San Pedro Playhouse can truthfully say that its origins stretch back to around 1858 when the Old Market House was first built many miles away in downtown San Antonio. The building, which was knocked down to make way for a river bypass, was to be the model of the playhouse. The intention was to move it from one site to where it currently stands, though the pieces were haphazardly thrown about with those from other buildings, making such a reconstruction impossible. In the end, the building was recreated essentially from photographs and willpower. The main artist in charge of the project was Gutzon Borglam, whose most famous creation was Mount Rushmore.

In 1930, the theater opened its doors with a production of "The Swan" to rave reviews and hoards of patrons. It continued steady operations until 1947 when World War II temporarily prompted the theater to go dark. Since that time, it has never gone dark again.

Although already inspiring in design and structure, it was the people involved in the playhouse who made it great. Beginning with the two artists who founded the San Antonio Conservation Society in order to save the building, it has been privileged with the influence of some truly great people. Sarah Barton Brimley, who founded the San Antonio Dramatic Club in 1912, was one of the first residents of the new theater, followed quickly by the Little Theater Producing Company of San Antonio. For more than eighty years, the San Pedro Playhouse has brought its tradition of entertainment to the public.

The Ghosts...

There is always a "ghost light," a single bulb left burning on the stage. According to some, its purpose is logical; without it the first to come in would enter the building in utter darkness. Still others claim that the light, for whatever reason, keeps the ghosts at bay.

According to Technical Director Paul Garza, there are numerous paranormal occurrences in the building. From noises on the shop floor to the image of someone walking down the stairs when the building is supposed to be empty, no one who spends any time in the San Pedro Playhouse doubts it to be haunted. Among the phenomena reported are lights that go on and off during shows, things misplaced or moved, and even the sensation of being watched. Most often, actors and technicians alike have seen apparitions of people in the audience, usually toward the back of the theater, when there should be no one there.

Reports of supernatural activity are not limited, however, to the main stage and backstage area. There is also a basement theater, called Cellar Theater, where people have reported seeing apparitions. A plume of smoke is how the apparitions are described...just appearing in mid air with neither spark nor flame to cause it. In one instance, a production was so plagued by paranormal activity, including the accidental injury to a lead actress, that the production crew would no longer say the name of the production, only referring to it as "that show."

As to who these spirits are, there are a few guesses. At least two of them, who have been sighted often, were a couple who loved the theater so much that, when they died, they had their cremated remains interred in the San Pedro Playhouse. Others are believed to be the spirits of actors and even people who just loved the theater. So many different phenomena occur in so many different places that current employees do not believe them all to be the work of just one or two entities.

Present Day

The year 2000 saw the theater refurbished, receiving updated lighting and sound systems, more advanced facilities, and renovated seating and lobby areas. It runs full theater seasons, offering musicals and other productions as well as experimental productions in the smaller Cellar Theater downstairs.

Paranormal activity is rather constant throughout the building, depending on what is going on and whether or not the resident entities take a liking to the current productions.

As the theater runs a full season, the best times to see the theater and its crew are during performances of one of their wonderfully produced shows. Auditions are held often for productions, and help is often needed in running the technical side of shows. Those wishing a paranormal experience, however, would be well advised to actually work in the theater, for, while some patrons have reported odd things, phenomena mostly happens during rehearsals and behind the scenes where most patrons just don't see. Becoming part of the production company seems like the best course of action, unless of course they are producing "that show."

For reservations, call 210-733-7258. More information about the theater can be found at its web site http://www.sanpedroplayhouse.com.

San Antonio Express News

**301 Avenue E
San Antonio, TX 78205**

San Antonio Express News

At night, the city sleeps. Even so, there are places that do not. Dedicated to the documentation of life, such places are manned by those who pursue the culture of a city. In the wee hours, however, it's not the city that is of concern, but the goings on within the walls. Phantom footsteps and cold breezes may not be the norm in most places, but here there are those who walk without the benefit of legs or even a pulse. Within the shadows, the past is as alive today as it was a century ago. Those who work in the offices and hallways of the building have a unique and rare privilege, to observe the past firsthand...*as the dead return to relive it.*

Newspapers are the lifeblood of any community. Not only do they report the news, they serve as the standing record of the city's history. By looking back at the old headlines, one can see the development of any community from its earliest moments to the present. But more than just report the history, newspapers actually are history in and of themselves. No other entity grows with a community as does a newspaper, and as it sees the development of a people, so too does it endure its tragedies. Within the hallowed walls, where history is not allowed to be forgotten, echoes from the past thrive. Whether in the form of former employees or glimpses back into time, the *San Antonio Express News* breathes the past and has the reputation of being haunted.

The History

In order to examine the history of the San Antonio Express News, one must consider three separate histories. First, there is the history of the newspaper itself. Second, the history of the city must be taken into account. Finally, the buildings must bear scrutiny, as all of these factors combine to create one of the most haunted locations in the city. While entire volumes could be written on the subject of the *San Antonio Express News*, there are a few key elements that bear investigation.

According to the official history of the paper, the *Express News* printed its first issue on September 27, 1865. It began as a weekly paper, competing with several other local papers that were printed in other languages. Of all the newspapers from the past, only the *San Antonio Express News* remains. The first editor was a judge named William Jones, whom the people nicknamed "fiery" for his temper and passion. He remained the editor for only a few months before turning the reins over to Major W. B. Moore.

Several years prior, in 1861, another newspaper existed, helmed by a man named James Newcomb. His paper, called the *Alamo Express*, was popular until, in 1861, Newcomb ran an editorial that portrayed him as siding with the Union forces.

Enraged, the citizens of San Antonio set his office on fire and drove him out of town. He returned in 1867 to assume the duties vacated by Moore. The impression he made was better this time around, it seemed, as he was appointed Texas Secretary of State, turning the editorial duties back over to Moore. It was not, however, his last attempt at journalism, as in 1881 he founded his own newspaper, the *San Antonio Light*.

Over its many years of operation, the *San Antonio Express News* has seen its share of memorable characters. One of them appeared in 1884 in the form of fifteen-year-old Frank Huntress. A paperboy, Huntress devised a system of delivery to the Fort Sam Houston area that tripled their circulation. It was an indicator of things to come for the young man. Less than thirty years later, the one-time paperboy rose to be the president and general manager of Express Publishing.

The year 1924 saw an interesting development in the battle for journalistic supremacy in San Antonio, as newspaper tycoon William Randolph Hearst purchased the *San Antonio Light*, setting up a war that would continue for more than seven decades. In the pages of the newspapers, the verbal sparring grew to a fevered pitch, at times degenerating to blatant name-calling and insults. When the *Express News* moved into a new building in 1929, it was followed in less than two years by a new building opening for the *Light*. That the *Express News* moved into its building of new prosperity on October 29 — the day the stock market crashed — was lost on no one.

Innovations also marked the life of the *San Antonio Express News*. While many involved the installation of state-of-the-art presses over the years, others were a bit less conventional. At almost the same time a new press was bought that could print 60,000 pages an hour, the paper also purchased a flock of eighty homing pigeons for the purpose of quick reporting at sporting events. Photographers would carry pigeons along to the events, then tie the film canisters to the birds' legs, ensuring their photos would arrive first.

San Antonio Express News (main building)

In 1973 Rupert Murdoch purchased the *San Antonio Express News*, bringing a new and wilder edge to the newspaper war. His flashy style was employed to pick up readers, using other innovations such as "Wingo," a bingo-style game with cash prizes, and a Sunday supplemental. Also, there were the sensationalist headlines that drew readers in by the score. Actual headline examples include "MIDGET ROBS UNDERTAKER AT MIDNIGHT!" and "VAMPIRE KILLER STALKS CITY!"

In 1984, the *San Antonio Express* merged with its sister publication, the *News*. It also saw the *San Antonio Express News* dominating the San Antonio market. Six years later, the history took a decidedly unexpected twist, as the Hearst Corporation, defeated in the newspaper game, closed the *Light* and bought the *San Antonio Express News*. It also purchased a pair of historic houses, the Flannery House and the Beversdorf House, for its operations. While the latter was never anything more than a small family home, the former had quite a history already. Built in 1899, the Flannery House first served as a boarding house for tourists. Thirty years later, it was purchased by the Catholic Women's Association as a boarding house for unwed mothers. From the 1940s until 1988, it served as a dorm for girls in the Catholic school.

The Ghosts...

Between the three buildings, there are more stories of odd happenings than at almost any other spot in San Antonio. From cold spots to full apparitions, the employees of the *San Antonio Express News* have seen it all. And while only a precious few phenomena have been identified, few can doubt that in the three buildings, history is alive.

By far, most of the phenomena are reported within the old Flannery House. There have been the sounds of footsteps on the old stairs without feet to accompany them and the scent of perfume filtering through the offices, accompanied by cool breezes. One employee, a retired Lieutenant Colonel, has had so many experiences in the building that he has come to expect them. There have been several reports of a strange mist that floats up the stairs, as well as voices that whisper to the workers who are there late at night.

There have also been two apparitions reported in the building. While one remains unidentified, the other is well known. According to Gus Gonzalez, who often gives tours of the buildings, a contributing editor named Maury Maverick worked for many years at the paper. He died on a Thursday night late in life. On Monday morning, however, Gonzalez was surprised to look down the hall and see the familiar old man walking to his office as always. Flabbergasted, he ran to catch up with him... only to find no one there.

The second apparition is believed to be from the time when young unwed mothers took up residency in the home. She is described as a woman dressed in a long white nurse's outfit. While several on the staff have seen her, her presence has never been considered hostile or threatening. There have also been reports of flashes of a past time, in which staff members will open the doors to their offices and see the rooms as they once were, with beds and dressers.

The other two buildings have a few stories, though not nearly as many as the Flannery house. In one building's storage area, people have reported seeing shadows darting about the size of children, as if they were playing hide and seek. In the area where the rolls of newsprint are stored, there have been frequent reports of a man in a suit who is simply seen walking as if going to an appointment. The old printing floor still has a lingering smell of hydraulic fluid, and people often speak of how they can still hear the old presses running. In one portion of the telecommunications rooms, people have reported being poked and pushed by unseen hands.

Present Day

The buildings occupied by the San Antonio Express News all serve their purposes. The Flannery House, for example, houses editorial staff and the paper's personnel offices. The main building is home to the General Manager, Xerox, circulation, and classified ads. One of the buildings occupied, on Broadway, actually used to be the home to the old *San Antonio Light* paper.

Still, disturbances continue. During one period of advancement, new presses were brought in that shook so violently when in use that it was feared they'd shake the building apart. To solve the problem, long columns were dug into the ground to support the machinery. While digging, the workers uncovered a small river, leading many to believe that Native Americans may have camped in the area, adding to the haunted folklore of the building. There are, to this day, some who will not go down into the sub basement area alone and others who do not like working the night shift. Some, however, take the activity in the building in stride.

As the *San Antonio Express News* is a very busy newspaper, the best time to visit is through a scheduled tour of the facility. As for places, the Flannery Home is a fascinating place whether or not a paranormal event occurs, as there are photos on the walls of the original newspaper staff and facilities. Other places are not generally open for public viewing.

To reach the main switchboard at the newspaper, call 210-250-3000. Offices are located at 301 Avenue E, 400 3rd Street, and 420 Broadway. Other contact information can be found at http://www.mysanantonio.com/.

Wolfson Manor

415 South Broadway
515 McCullough Avenue (church)
San Antonio, TX 78215

Wofson Manor

The image of the haunted house is cliché, with craggy peaks, pointed roofs, and shadows that run long around it. Victorian architecture often lends itself to the imaginative, believing that the eaves jut like fangs, that the windows glint like eyes, and that the front door is a gaping maw from which there is no escape. In most cases, however, houses that look haunted simply aren't, instead the victims of fanciful wishes and overactive imaginations. But for every cliché, there is a cause; an event before it became the overused joke. While the front door may not bear teeth and there may be nothing malevolent about it, sometimes the house that looks haunted *is* haunted. And for those with a strong enough imagination, such a place doesn't merely exist...*it breathes*....

There are many types of hauntings, so many in fact that cataloging all the different phenomena would require a ponderous volume. In some, a horrific death causes restless souls to replay their last moments. In others, the apparitions are nothing more than a memory, an echo in time. Still others are caused by nothing short of a deep love of a place or thing, providing a lasting imprint on it. Such a haunting can be attached to something as small as a silver box or as large as a house, letting that feeling of love come through for anyone who experiences it. While there are many names for that feeling of warmth, such a presence is most often described, by those who feel it, as a welcoming presence, a benevolent spirit, or simply by saying the place or object is haunted.

The History

In 1888, a Prussian dry-goods salesman named Saul Wolfson came to San Antonio and opened a store on Main Plaza. For his family, he built a home, the likes of which is not seen anywhere else in the city. At 5,042 square feet of living space, the gargantuan structure contained eight fireplaces, vaulted ceilings, and rolled glass windows, completing a picture of elegance that few could match in the time and none can match now. The back of the home extended to the San Antonio River, which the family used for disposing household garbage.

Saul Wolfson lived in the house with his wife, Emelia, and four sons, Abe, Emil, Milton, and Jesse. As his boys grew older and found homes of their own, Wolfson began to use various rooms in the house as office space, bringing in books and files and even a walk-in safe. The safe was later converted into the world's most secure shower.

When he died in 1923, he left the house to his wife who, in turn, left the building to their four sons. It was Abe that lived in the house for quite some time before selling it to Mrs. Chester Webb, for whom the home doubled as an antique gallery. It was during her time in the house that a great deal of restoration occurred, uncovering many unexpected treasures. Hidden in one wall was a box marked "wash woman" that contained a silver place setting for eight. Also discovered was a small silver box with a note inside, presumably for Emelia Wolfson from Saul, which read: "Darling, would you please put your rings in this little box instead of on the floor." It was also during this time that the first rumors of restless spirits began to emerge.

Mrs. Webb lived in the home until 1979, when public record shows the home belonged to Warren Reed as offices for his advertising business. The First Baptist Church of San Antonio purchased it in 1982.

The Ghosts...

While few have seen her, there is little doubt as to the identity of the person who haunts the hallways of her beloved house. It's the considered opinion of those who have owned the home that Emelia Wolfson loved the house her husband built so much that she simply never left, and is the cause of some very interesting phenomena.

One of the more common events is the sound of footsteps walking through the building when it is otherwise empty. They have been reported to occur during both daytime and nighttime hours by all the former owners. Also reported have been objects moving by themselves. In one instance, a painting of Emelia Wolfson moved itself over and over again until it was displayed in a place of prominence. In another, a former owner and two of her friends actually watched a curio cabinet lift off the floor, travel across the room, and settle without breaking or damaging any of the objects held inside.

Most often felt, it is the apparition that is sometime seen that provides the identity of the restless soul. Described as a small woman with grey hair, she has been identified from photos as Emelia Wolfson. She is most often witnessed moving from room to room downstairs, dissipating when encountered by the living.

Present Day

Though the old back porch was removed and replaced by a deck and window air conditioners have been added, the house is largely as Wolfson left it. True, the wiring is new and it has been re-roofed, but as a fine example to bygone craftsmanship it has no equal. The home is currently used by the church for Sunday School classes and special events, and is the site of their once-a-year craft show.

Though it's been a while since she's been seen by anyone on the church staff, there are still those who feel Mrs. Wolfson's presence. Also, a few employees of the *San Antonio Express News,* located across from the house, have mentioned seeing an old woman waving to them from one of the upstairs rooms. Whether or not it's Mrs. Wolfson is unknown, but the general consensus is that she's not malevolent in any way—she simply loved her house too much to leave it.

There is no way of knowing when, or if, Mrs. Wolfson will appear again. Her manifestations seemed to intensify around the time of renovation and slowly tapered off through the years. Still, it is believed that she still lingers in the house. For those who want to see the house and marvel at the architecture, the best way is to either attend the Sunday School classes held there or to plan to attend the annual craft show.

For more information, call the church's main number, 210-226-0363, or visit its web site at http://www.fbcsa.org.

La Villita

South Alamo at Nueva
418 Villita Street (main office)
Suite 900
San Antonio, TX 78205

Entrance to La Villita

he stone steps and adobe walls are an anachronism, something out of time and out of place in the modern world. Still, they stand, attracting visitors from all over the world. Those who work here are sort of family, with many of them having been here for more than thirty years. Here they work...and some have died. And yet...*they do not leave*. Even before them, others were here. Before they were shops and restaurants, these adobe buildings were homes. Families made their lives here. While many make their living here now, those who came before, in many cases, refuse to be forgotten. While most see them as protective spirits—

beings that give the tight-knit community its life—few can deny that the dead still walk the stone ways. *No matter what now sits in the buildings here, the dead will always call it home.*

Every place has a history. No matter what exists there now, something existed before, whether it was empty land or a battlefield, a hospital or boarding house. Often, shops and restaurants feel the spirits of the past intruding on present time, reminding the proprietors of the history of their establishments. In fact, it's common for many shops in an historic town such as San Antonio to have paranormal activity. Yet, when the site of a haunting is not just a shop or restaurant–*but an entire village*–the scope of the haunting changes. It goes from being an isolated event to a community phenomenon. Just talking to the proprietors of the shops in San Antonio's historic La Villita (The Little Village) reveals a complex history that has grown and changed with the city.

The History

When San Antonio was young, the missions were built by the Catholic Church to spread the word of God. By 1792, the missions had been secularized and there became a need for other types of structures. Built nearly in the shadow of what is now known as The Alamo, such a structure came in the form of a tiny village of huts for Spanish soldiers and their families. This collection became known as La Villita, or "The Little Village."

In the beginning, the homes were mostly constructed of straw and wood, but a flood in 1819 decimated the village. New structures were put up, this time of much sturdier materials. Homes of straw were replaced with brick and adobe. By 1836, the Little Village had recovered and grown to outgrow the "little" part of its name. Immigrants from Germany and France arrived, adding their own cultural flair to the community and influencing the architecture. The Little Village, however, began a slow decline into poverty.

According to a tour brochure handed out at La Villita, there are more than twenty-five structures in the tiny community, most of which date back to as early as 1835. In addition to the various private homes, there are quite a few places of historic note. The Cos House, for example, was where General Perfecto de Cos signed the articles of Capitulation in 1835 after being handed defeat by the Texans.

In 1929, the United States fell into the Great Depression and San Antonio was among the places hit hardest. The Little Village became a slum, with many of the buildings deteriorating into decay and others becoming the site for less than savory activities. It looked as though La Villita was going to be destroyed, if not by the wrecking ball than its own poverty. However, in 1939, something that could be considered a miracle happened.

Franklin D. Roosevelt, then President, instituted his New Deal as a way to help put Americans back to work and pull the country out of economic ruin. One of his programs, the National Youth Administration, was designed to teach young people trades to get them out of hopeless poverty. At the same time, San Antonio's mayor, Maury Maverick, had the idea to restore and preserve the little town. With an army of youngsters, the mayor began sweeping changes that altered the state of La Villita and ensured that it would not be lost to vandals. A kitchen building was constructed to feed the restoration workers, as was a kiln for the arts and crafts programs that created the clay tiles for the streets and floors. In the 1960s, La Villita was again in danger, as much of the land around it was being swept up to prepare for Hemisfair. Staunch political support for the Little Village stemmed the tide, however, and saved the buildings.

Of note are the histories of several buildings, which one must cross-reference on two separate maps to see what is what today. One house, which was originally used to house the New York Star Cleaning and Dye Works, later was leased by the Joy Kist Candy Company and then became a house of ill repute. Also owned by both the candy company and the brothel was the Esquida/Downs/Dietrich house across the street. The McAllister House and Store was a dry-goods shop until it was incorporated into the Little Village in 1949. Many of the other buildings were private homes that housed various businesses over the years.

The Ghosts...

With twenty-seven structures, including a church and several taverns, one would think there would be at least a few restless souls hanging about. And one would be absolutely correct. It is not surprising to note that not all of the resident spirits of La Villita come from its distant past, but seem to be from those who until recently dwelled within her walls.

There was, at one time, a resident Starving Artist named Jesse Sanchez who lived at La Villita and reported seeing a woman in a long white dress walking after-hours behind the little church. The same apparition has been sighted by several of the shop owners and employees, although her identity has never been determined. She has been seen not only near the church, but also on the porch of what was once called the Florian House, the present location of River Art Group.

Next to the Little Church is a building that now houses Chamade Jewelers, whose employees have had several experiences with whom they believe are a woman and her children who still seem to inhabit the building. As the home was at one point a school and then a home for unwed mothers, it has seen its share of emotional turmoil. She's often seen as a moving shadow at closing times and has whispered the names of Chamade Jewelers' employees, who believe her to be a protective soul.

Another reported site of paranormal activity is a house that was disassembled from its original location on the Hemisfair grounds and reassembled in the La Villita community. Now home to a fine arts and custom framing at Artistic Endeavors, the building seems to have at least a few resident specters. According to owner Denise Barron, who is also the head of the tenants' association, fleeting shadows zip through the shop, and there have been numerous cases in which items have been moved and dropped around the shop. Docia Williams related a story in her book *When Darkness Falls* about the house, in which the spirit of a little girl revealed the location of a hidden treasure in the fireplace—a bundle containing a wedding gown, money, and a bit of jewelry. When the house was moved from its original location because of Hemisfair, construction workers found the bundle. Although the discovery was documented, no one seems to know what happened to the pieces.

Not every ghost in La Villita is from distant time periods. At least one is a recent development. Bolivar Cafe, located in the former Bolivar Hall, reportedly receives visits from "Tiny," who used to own the cafe, from time to time. While some are skeptical about his presence, several other shopkeepers believe he loved La Villita so much that he never left.

Present Day

La Villita today is a haven for artists and artisans, and does a brisk business on most days. Many of the businesses have been in operation for more than thirty years, making conversations with the shopkeepers a fascinating look into history. No matter the year, La Villita seems to be charmed, as the citizens of San Antonio have, on several occasions, come to its aid in time of need. While a few of the shopkeepers report having no paranormal experiences whatsoever, others declare that activity is an almost daily occurrence.

There is a theory that paranormal activity occurs all the time at La Villita, but it's such a busy place that no one notices until after-hours. Nonetheless, there are at least a few who will not venture inside the walls after the sun has fallen. The best places to visit are purely subjective to a person's tastes, except to say that not one shop should be missed. It seems that the best time of year to visit is during the early spring and autumn months when the Texas heat won't spoil the experience.

For more information, contact the Main Office at 210-207-8610 or visit its web site at http://www.lavillita.com.

Urban Legends & Lost Treasures

Throughout the nation, there are stories of horrific happenings. Madmen, weeping women, phantom hitchhikers, and torn lovers are often the subjects, serving as cautionary tales for anyone who might hear them. No matter how resonating the story, however, many of them can be proven, with little research, to be wholly untrue. Most often, these stories can be found repeated, with few differences, all across the world, and those that tell them believe to the core of their being that they are true. Whether the story comes from the friend of a girlfriend of a twice-removed cousin or was something that someone thinks they remember "seeing on the news one time," these stories are called "Urban Legends."

Still, there are stories that seem too fantastic, too far-fetched to be true, and yet are more than mere fantasy. Stories about men in rabbit costumes, such as in the famed Bunnyman Bridge of Clifton, Virginia, may seem laughable, but are chilling in a whole different way when research proves the subjects to be real. Searching for these locations proves oftentimes difficult, leading to empty fields or apartments, housing developments or strip malls. But, according to newspapers, city records, and police reports, they once did exist. Whether lost to time or the developer's wrecking ball, the stories continue to be told, and their memories deserve to be honored as well.

The Ghost Tracks of San Antonio

Urban Legend

For more than fifty years, usually on Halloween, people flock to a certain area of Stan Antonio and park on an otherwise innocuous set of railroad tracks. Suicide is not on their agenda, nor is causing a train wreck. Rather, they are there to see if the legends are true, if the dead do walk, and if the restless souls of children will push their cars uphill and off the tracks.

According to legend, the children perished in a tragic accident in the 1930s when their bus stalled on the train tracks. A train, traveling at full speed, struck the bus, crushing it and killing everyone aboard. The numbers often change, putting the death toll sometimes at more than twenty, sometimes at only around five. In response to the tragedy, the city mourned. The surrounding streets were renamed to reflect the names of the children killed.

Those who tell the story often point to the streets that bear names such as "Bobbie-Sue Lane" and "Stevie Street" (not their real names) as proof that the event really happened. Furthermore, they all seem to know someone who knows someone who knew a child killed in the accident. Most importantly, these people will then park their cars across the tracks, turn off the engines, and put their car into "neutral." What happens next can be disconcerting, if not astonishing.

No one knows who first noticed the phenomena, but thousands have experienced it over the years. Inside the car, the passengers feel the vehicle begin to move, slowly at first, but picking up speed. A glance out the window reveals that, although there is nothing behind it, the car is indeed moving—and appears to be moving uphill. Once across the tracks, the car slows to a halt. Across the trunk, where the teller has sprinkled baby powder, appears to be handprints where invisible fingers have pushed the vehicle to safety. The legend, it appears, is true.

Or is it? Do the ghosts of dead children stand guard over the tracks that took their lives, rescuing those who tempt fate? The reality is far less romantic than phantom children, and some quick research can shed light on the issue. According to the web site Snopes, the resource for debunking nearly every urban legend there is, there was a bus that stalled on a set of railroad tracks resulting in the deaths of twenty-six children in 1938—IN Utah. Despite claims to the contrary, no such accident ever occurred in San Antonio. The event was, however, considered a national tragedy, and was front-page news all across the nation, but as America mourned, an urban legend developed in the minds of those who remembered the tragedy, but were too young to remember the details. An entire generation bore witness to the front-page news, but did not read the rest of the story. In their minds, for such a tragedy to have occurred and have had such an impact, it must surely have been a local event.

But what of the street names? Don't they prove the veracity of the story? Surely the names of the children on the street signs are proof positive of a mourning city. On the contrary, the streets surrounding the site that bear the names of children were, in fact, named for the children and grandchildren of the gentleman who planned that particular subdivision, and they are, as of this writing, all alive and well. But what about the phenomenon of the car rolling uphill, aided by unseen hands?

Debunking this legend is a simple matter. A carpenter's level, when placed on the tracks, reveals the "uphill" slope is actually an optical illusion and is, in fact, going downhill. The vehicle is, in fact, just aided by gravity, not diminutive spirits. As to the handprints on the trunk, most likely they were there to begin with, just unnoticed, or tricks of dirt and moisture. In many cases, the prints are proven to belong to the vehicle's owner.

Despite repeated debunking by both the press and ghost hunters, this urban legend persists, leading hundreds to tie up traffic at the dubiously famous tracks and annoying those who live in the vicinity and who are trying to do nothing more than get on with their daily lives. It's for this reason, and out of respect for the tracks' neighbors, that the actual location of the tracks is not included in this article.

The Legend of La Llorona

Urban Legend

t's late at night on the city streets. Shops have long since closed and bars have signaled "last call," prompting a steady stream of patrons out the door. When the neon lights stop flickering and the doors have been locked, the San Antonio streets are, for the most part, quiet. But there are nights when the darkness is troubled, disturbed by the sounds of a woman crying at the river's edge. Just who she was is heavily debated, but her purpose remains the same. Tonight, as she does for all eternity, she looks for her child whom she drowned in the river so many years ago, damning herself to an eternity of sorrow. She has been called by many names, but there is always one by which she is known: La Llorona, the weeping woman.

While many claim to have seen the mysterious lady in white by the river, her origins are as varied as the many names by which she goes. Some claim she was a poor working-class girl, impregnated and abandoned by her rich boyfriend. Others say she was prostitute, crazed in attempting to trap a wealthy man into marriage. In a third version of the story, she was a woman who was pregnant and was accused of cheating on her husband. Whatever the case, the end result of the stories are the same. In an attempt to exact revenge on those who had wronged her, she drowned her own child in the river, and then spent the rest of her life mourning the loss at the river's edge. Still another version of the story speaks of twin sisters who were so identical that, due to a mistake at a church, one was baptized twice while the other was not. The un-baptized one grew up to be loveless, drowning her children in the river. Perhaps the most tragic version reveals the spirit to be that of a fifteen-year-old girl who became pregnant without ever having known a man. In this case, it was her father who drowned the child, leaving the young woman to bleed to death on the riverbank.

Just as mysterious as her origin are the consequences of seeing her or hearing her cry. According to some versions of the legend, her wails are seen as a harbinger of misfortune, a Hispanic version of a Banshee. Her mournful wail has been said to foretell everything from the death of a loved one to natural disasters. Others point to the spirit as the stealer of children who stray too far from their parents, claiming she so misses her own child that she will claim any she finds. Some even credit her with spiriting away and disposing of husbands that cheat on their wives, hearkening back to at least two of the original legends. However, such claims seem only to further the cautionary aspects of the story, much the same as are with any urban legend.

While she has been sighted from as far north as Minnesota to as far south as Peru, as far east as Maine to as far west as California, the tale of her origin remains strangely constant. Research done by Anthropologist Bernadine Santistevan shows the earliest known reference to the weeping spirit as a goddess who weeps for the future of her "children," the Aztecs, in 1502. Furthermore, Santistevan's research also provides the possible true origin of the legend in the name La Malinche, an Aztec girl who fell in love with the conqueror Cortez, and who bore him two sons. Upon learning of his plan to return to Spain with his children, but without Malinche, she killed them both in the river. For the next ten years, she was seen grieving her decision by the banks of the river until her own death.

Other instances in history have created similar specters, creating a phenomenon known as the "woman in white." White-clad spirits are reported all across the world and are usually connected with some form of deep sorrow. Why these seemingly unrelated spirits all appear in similar dress is unknown and a topic for discussion wherever paranormal enthusiasts meet.

Whether the story of La Malinche is true or not, or whether it's the source of the legend, is subject for debate. However, La Llorona continues to be a rich part of San Antonio's folklore, as many claim to have seen her, and still more, whether having seen her or not, believe.

Midget Mansion

Lost Treasure

here are some stories that are told that are obvious bunk. Even those who routinely believe every urban legend can easily pick out certain tales as being pure hogwash because they're either just too fantastic, outlandish, or just plain unbelievable. Occasionally, however, there comes a story that fits the description of "so outlandish it can't be true" that turns out to be verifiable. While the details may be sketchy, and while the tellers may find themselves repeatedly swearing to the veracity of the story, doubters will find themselves on the losing end of the bet. Such a story exists in the legend of San Antonio's Midget Mansion.

Built in the early 1920s, this building came into the possession of a businessman who, in today's politically correct atmosphere, would be referred to as a "little person." His wife was similarly diminutive, though their children were, according to legend, normal sized. More than a dozen sources tell an identical story, one so bizarre that, true or not, is the stuff of campfire legends.

As with many urban legends, the businessman came home one day and, without so much as a greeting, stabbed his wife and sons and stuffed them into a closet in the house. A few days went by before he retrieved their bodies, cleaned and dressed them, replaced them in the closet, and then promptly hung (or shot, depending on the version of the story) himself. According to legend, the police found bloody handprints inside the closet door, indicating that the family may not have been quite dead when he stuffed them inside. Subsequent owners of the house were reputed to have heard scratching from inside the walls and wailing at night, prompting the house to be abandoned for many years, and giving it the stigma of being haunted.

By this time, the listeners are crying foul and snickering at how ridiculous a story it seems to be. A midget mass murderer and a mansion? Surely such a thing has never existed. If it had, it would have made national headlines, right? That is, of course, until the teller leads them to the burned out ruins of the house itself. The house, it seems, was real enough. Scanning message boards, searching the Internet, and reading past articles and books reveal the place to be one where many a San Antonio native visited as a rite of passage, a way to scare the dickens out of themselves, while looking for phantom little people. Reputed for a while to be a place where "Satanic" cults (which actually were just bored teens lashing out at their parents) practiced, it was just the sort of place to get a cheap thrill and boast of bravery while the imagination took over, amplifying every sound and darkening every shadow. Haunted or not, the place was genuinely creepy.

As time passed, so did the Midget Mansion. It was burned to the ground by those same bored youths, the swimming pool filled with concrete, and the fence around the place locked, waiting for a developer to buy the land. When development of an apartment complex began, failing memories and misdirection began to surface, sending people to the wrong location of the former mansion. It seemed that a genuine place would slip into the realm of the urban legend forever. However, a bit of research and luck shows the site's location to be the address of the Promontory Pointe apartment complex. While the residents themselves may have a few stories to tell, there seems to be no stories relating the supposed haunting of the mansion to the buildings now on its former property, nor have there been any reports of unexplained wall scratching or phantom little people re-enacting heinous crimes. The mansion, it seems, was lost forever.

Hot Wells Hotel & Resort

Lost Treasure

San Antonio has a rich history filled with royalty, stars, military giants, and Presidents. Many of the places where these titans walked have been enshrined, the adventures of those heroes of ages past becoming the stuff of legend. At least one place, however, through no fault of its own or even those who owned it, has all but disappeared, its history now visible only in a few crumbling walls and newspaper accounts. Ask enough of the older residents of San Antonio and their memories paint a vivid portrait of the once-proud structure called the Hot Wells Hotel & Resort.

There are conflicting reports of just when the hotel was originally built, but the fact remains that it was an entrepreneur named McClellan Shacklett who first had the idea to lease the sulfurous waters that bubbled up on the property and create a health resort. By 1892, Shacklett had created what became known as a world-class health spa and resort where the rich and famous came to soak in the sulfur waters, believing in their medicinal virtues. Pumped into baths and pools, the Edwards Aquifer-provided elixir attracted the likes of Charlie Chaplin, Teddy Roosevelt, Tom Mix, and Rudolph Valentino. So many stars came to stay at the resort that a film company, Star Film Ranch, based its operations out of the hotel for two years.

The hotel began floundering after 1911, but it was in 1919 that Prohibition fairly destroyed the business. In 1923, the hotel sold to the Christian Science Congregation, whose intent was to convert the whole structure into a school. It was not meant to be, however, as a fire sparked and burned down all but the bathhouse on the property. During the Great Depression of the 1930s, a cluster of bungalows was erected, some right on the foundations of the other buildings, for the purpose of turning the place into a tourist attraction. The springs still flowed, so people were allowed to come and bathe in the warm sulfur water. By 1942, it was a motor hotel and trailer park.

In 1979, an investor bought the property with dreams of turning it into a natural health and medicine spa. Renovations began, but were stopped in 1988 when lightning struck the tower on the property, once again burning large portions to the ground. In 1994, the property was taken over by the city for unpaid taxes; three years later, arson claimed still more of the property. It seemed as if the old hotel was doomed.

In 1999, however, James Lifshutz purchased the property at auction. Unsure of what to do with it, only that it had to be saved as a part of San Antonio's history, he began a slow process of petitioning the city for aid and cleaning up the land.

There have been many opinions as to what it should become. While some say just to bulldoze it and make way for something else, Lifshutz is adamant that it should be preserved. Among the ideas bounced around for its purpose has been as an artist colony to reopening it as an old-fashioned health spa, with no real decisions made. One thing is for certain, however. According to an interview from 2005, Lifshutz says that as long as he owns the property, it's safe from being completely destroyed.

As for ghosts, it's easy to explain the "putrid stench of death" that many report as the natural aroma of sulfur-infused hot water. What is not so easy to explain, however, are the stories of voices heard, feelings of being watched or followed, and unexplainable cold spots in open ground. Says Lifshutz, "As far as odd things having happened at Hot Wells, its entire history has evolved around odd things: miracle cures from the magic of the healing waters, Judge Roy Bean's gifting a mountain lion to the menagerie there, ostrich races, Teddy Roosevelt's Rough Riders drinkin' and whorein' there during the tenth anniversary of the Battle of San Juan Hill, Gloria Swanson's swimming lessons, etc. As for the paranormal, the only spirits that we've heard of or found there have been benevolent spirits — but we've been unable to identify them more specifically." With any luck, Mr. Lifshutz will be able to preserve this piece of San Antonio's history.

References

Alma Cross of the Bullis House Inn Bed & Breakfast

Amy Fulkerson, Collections Manager, Witte Museum

Art Link of Columns on Alamo Bed & Breakfast

Bill Brindle, of the Emily Morgan Hotel

Bradford A. Johnson

Darrell Beauchamp, Executive Director of the National Western Art Foundation

David Rodriguez of the Westin Hotel on Market Street

De Zavala, Adina. *History and Legends of the Alamo and Other Missions In and Around San Antonio*. Houston, Texas: Arte Publico Press, 1996.

Debbie Gonzalez of the Sheraton Gunter Hotel

Deborah Martin of San Antonio College

Dianne Smilgin of Terrell Castle Inn

Docia Schultz Williams, San Antonio's ghost expert

Dr. Rosalind Rock, Historian

Ernesto Malacara of the Menger Hotel

Gus Gonzalez, Jr., Jerry Salazar, Louis Alonzo, and Manuel Martinez of the *San Antonio Express News*

Habig, Marion A. OFM. *The Alamo Chain of Missions*. Chicago, Illinois: Franciscan Herald Press, 1968.

Heather McCrocklin of CSPR

http://www.lallorona.com/La_index.html

http://www.snopes.com/horrors/ghosts/handprint.asp

http://www.theshadowlands.com/places/texas.htm

James Lifshutz of the Lifshutz Companies

James Rowe of the St. Anthony Hotel

Jennifer C. Johnson

Jesse Medina, owner, the Cadillac Bar Restaurant

Joan Williams of the McAllister Auditorium, San Antonio College

Jonathan Filoteo of the Menger Hotel

Margaret Hadley of the First Baptist Church of San Antonio

Megan MacDaniel of the Oge House

Paul Garza of the San Pedro Playhouse

Paul, Lee. "La Llorona." http://www.theoutlaws.com and "Legends of the Alamo." www.theoutlaws.com

Rhett Rushing of The Institute for Texan Cultures

Ron Springate of First Baptist Church of San Antonio

Sarah Padilla of San Antonio College

Shannon Standley, Manager of Public Relations, Witte Museum

Shirley Dyer, of the Crockett Hotel

Stacy Beach of the Briscoe Museum

The San Antonio Botanical Gardens Staff

Tiffany Wheiles

Vicci of the Church Bistro & Theater at King William

Victor Cortez of the St. Anthony Hotel

Villalobos, Brian. "Man Seeks Ghost." *San Antonio Current*, January 3, 2007.

Williams, Docia Schultz. *History and Mystery of the Menger Hotel*. San Antonio, Texas: Republic of Texas Press, 2000. *When Darkness Falls: Tales of San Antonio Ghosts and Hauntings.* San Antonio, Texas: Republic of Texas Press, 1997.

Williams, Docia Schultz and Reneta Byrne. *Spirits of San Antonio and South Texas*. San Antonio, Texas: Republic of Texas Press, 1992.